Because They're Assholes

Assholes

Violence and Gun Violence

by

Michael R. Weisser

in collaboration with

William A. Weisser

Volume 3 of 4 Volumes: Guns in America

Published by:

TeeTee Press
Ware MA 01082

Cover design by Damonza

ISBN: 0692215573
ISBN-13: 978-0692215579

10 9 8 7 6 5 4 3 2 1

First Edition

To the memory of William Earl Weisser
March 7, 1942 – October 30, 1962

ALSO BY MICHAEL R. WEISSER

The Peasants of the Montes: Roots of Revolution in Spain

Crime and Punishment in Early Modern Europe

A Brotherhood of Memory: Jewish Landsmanshaftn in the New World

Guns for Good Guys, Guns for Bad Guys: Gun Violence in America

Hunters in the Wilderness: Opening and Closing the Frontier

CONTENTS

CHAPTER 1

WHAT IS GUN VIOLENCE?

In the town down the road from where I live there was a nineteen or twenty year-old kid named Lenny living with his mother. He was thought to be gay but not in a particularly flagrant or obvious sort of way. On the other hand, his one best friend, a Puerto Rican kid about the same age, went around town playing up his homosexuality both in word and deed. One night the two kids drove out to the isolated house of Lenny's great uncle, an octogenarian who lived alone, bopped the old man over the head, shot him four or five times with his own gun for good measure, then dragged the corpse a half-mile into the woods and dumped it into a shallow grave.

It took the cops less than two days to figure the whole thing out, largely because Lenny and his friend Rafael left enough clues and forensic evidence for law enforcement to make the case with their eyes shut. Between paperwork, warrants, affidavits and an argument between two prosecutors over whether the kids would be charged in the town where the murder took place or the town where the body was found (the two geniuses had inadvertently dragged the old man's corpse across a town line before rolling him into the ditch), it took four times as long for the cops to arrest the kids as it took them to figure out who committed the crime.

Neither kid had any kind of a real criminal record, nor had they been particularly difficult or considered discipline problems in school. There was nothing in their backgrounds or behavior that would predict that they were capable of committing a really fiendish crime. And when Lenny was questioned as to the reasons for murdering the old man, he said something to the effect that they went up to the house to steal some money, found the guy sitting around and figured that dead men can't talk, so take the loot but don't leave a witness behind. The loot turned out to be less than fifty bucks. The old man was worth fifty bucks.

Several days after the case was solved I had a chance to talk with the police chief in my town. He's been a chief for more than twenty years, runs a well-managed department on a shoestring budget and does a very good job. After he told me the ins and outs of the case, I asked him why he thought these two kids would commit such a terrible and meaningless crime.

After all, I said, they didn't have reputations for being tough or brutal kids. And it wasn't as if they divvied up a big score. "You know what?" he answered. "They did it because they're assholes."

I thought about the Chief's answer many times while I was doing the research for this book. And in a funny kind of way, as simplistic as it sounded, now that I've finished it his answer makes a lot of sense. Because violence of that sort is senseless and incapable of being explained or understood in any rational terms. There's no logic, no coherence, no plan. The two brats showed up on the old man's doorstep, whacked him over the head, pumped him full of holes, dumped the body into a ditch and went away. On their way back into town they stopped off and shared a cheese pizza, with Lenny taking the few uneaten slices back home to his Mom. The cops questioned the guy who sold them the pizza. The cops question everybody. That's what they do.

I should add that the case was solved because when the two assholes left the old man's property, one of them drove back into town in the car in which they had gone out to the old man's place, the other for some unaccountable reason drove back into town in the victim's van. The latter vehicle was stashed in the parking area of the town's senior center and the driver, one of the two assholes, was seen alighting from the van when a security tape of the parking area was reviewed the next day. The cops took a look at the tape, took a look at it again, then went out and grabbed the kids. A really tough case to close.

Now I want to tell you about *my* first encounter with violence. I was twelve and my brother, to whom this volume is dedicated, took me to the Museum of Modern Art in New York City to see a one-person exhibition of photographs by a Jewish immigrant named Arthur Fellig who used the name "Weegee" on all his work. Weegee's photos (see one below) were a catalog of the seamy side of urban life, in particular grisly murder scenes that looked particularly grimy and dirty when taken at night. I can recall today, more than fifty years ago, how shocked and scared I felt looking at pictures of these brutally dead men and some women lying in the street. But I was also fascinated by what I saw; fascinated by the violence, by the blood, by the nonchalant looks on the cops and the EMT crews who had seen it all before. I had no idea that someday I would write a book that sought to explain what Weegee captured so brilliantly with his Speed Graphic camera and his wholly original technique. Are you ready? Let's begin.

WeeGee – Murder in Manhattan

This is the third of four volumes that I am writing about guns and, like the previous two volumes, I'm going to try to keep the text as concise as possible and the notes few and sparse in between. On the other hand, lack of footnotes doesn't mean lack of data. Like my other books, you can be sure that there is available data for every factual assumption or argument that I make. And nobody that I ever met was all that interested in going back and forth between text and footnotes anyway. But in case you're interested, you will find notes at the end of each chapter and some suggestions for further reading at the end of the entire text.

This volume also contains material that will not be enjoyable or easy to read. Because the truth is that violence simply isn't very pleasant, and the kinds of people who either commit it or are its victims usually aren't going to wind up at the top of your next dinner invitation list. I could have made this book the first volume in the series, but I wanted my readers, like yourself, to trust what I'm telling you, so I figured it would be better to gradually ease into some of the more controversial issues that are treated in this volume rather than putting it all out front and asking you to accept what I say on blind faith. If you've read either of the other volumes, you'll appreciate my decision to hold off discussing some of these issues in detail until now.

I have learned to look at violence, particularly gun violence, from two very different perspectives. On the one hand, there's the immediate and inexplicable event, the kind of behavior represented by kids like Lenny and Rafael who didn't even need a split second to think about what they were going to do. Nor did they have a history of engaging in violence of this or any sort. But they stood in front of the old man one second and the old guy's brains were splattered all over the couch in the next. There's a lot of gun violence out there, perhaps a majority of all shootings, which happens in this way.

But there's also the other side, the gun violence that represents an escalation of what had been a less-lethal pattern of violence, in which the decision to use a gun means that the argument or the conflict is going to come to an end. And it's not just about ending the argument. It's also about adding an additional element to the anger that erupted when the argument first began. Get yourself into an ER or Trauma Unit the next time a shooting victim is wheeled in. All of a sudden the place becomes hell's bells as everyone starts running, yelling, cutting, attaching, frantically and frenetically trying to stop a living person from abandoning life and sliding into death. But while the doctors and other ER personnel are working on the victim, pumping his chest, running lines, anything and everything at the same time, they may also be talking to the patient because they know him, they've seen him before, he came in last week or last month with other trauma injuries that didn't involve a gun.

You can't think about gun violence without thinking about violence, and violence happens all the time. It's a lot more common than gun violence which as a crime statistic is relatively rare. But violence and gun violence exist side by side and if anyone thinks there's some plan out there that will deal with one without dealing with the other, they don't know anything about violence and they don't know anything about guns. Which is the point of this book: to talk about violence and talk about guns. But before we talk about either one, there's a very important point that I want to make.

Violence is a form of behavior. Doesn't matter where or when or how it takes place, it's still a behavioral phenomenon. And gun violence is a particularly destructive and often lethal form of this behavior, a particularly deadly sub-category of this type of behavior. What makes gun violence so difficult to understand is not just that it is a form of behavior, and behavior is always difficult to understand. There's something more. And that something is what this book is really all about, namely, the extent to which gun violence is a very *impulsive* form of behavior. And I am not sure if many of the people who engage in this form of behavior in an impulsive manner necessarily understand the connection between what they are about to do and the result of what they end up doing.

So let's begin with a definition. What do we mean when we use the term "gun violence?" I am a firearms trainer, certified by the National Rifle Association and the Massachusetts State Police, and when I use the term "gun violence" I am talking about using a gun for purposes other than for what it was intended to be used for, or what I call "unauthorized' use. In other words, if someone walks into my shop and asks, "What's the best gun for me to buy so that I can shoot my wife?" I will break out laughing, but if he doesn't immediately join in I won't sell him a gun. And if he tells me he's serious, I'll pick up the phone and call the police.

The one thing about gun violence that makes it a singular form of violence is the fact that it is *definitive*, both in terms of its result as well as its possible result. There simply isn't another way to commit violence which is as immediate, as efficient and, most of all, as reliable as using a gun. If it goes off, which it almost always does, and the bullet hits someone, which it sometimes does, they are really going to be hurt. And that's the whole point of violence, isn't it? After all, no matter whether an act of violence is intended or not, whether it is committed with premeditation or not, whether the person who commits it understands or even thinks about the possible result, we define violence as an event that causes damage to someone else. So when we use the phrase *gun violence*, we are referring either to people getting hurt or possibly getting hurt. And the degree of hurt that can be suffered with a gun is much greater than the degree of hurt that usually occurs if we find some other way to damage ourselves or damage someone else.

There was a study in some Western states over the past few years that estimated the costs of gun violence compared to the costs of other types of injuries.[1] The researchers gathered data from emergency and trauma centers in Colorado, Washington, Oregon and California and computed gun injury treatment costs versus other serious trauma

9

like vehicular accidents, blunt and sharp instrument wounds (clubs and knives), serious falls, and so forth. They weren't comparing gunshots to hangnails. What they learned was that the cost of treating wounds from guns was 30% to 40% higher than any other type of serious injury because the medical response was not only much greater in terms of specific remedies, the amount of post-trauma convalescent time was also significantly higher. And the study didn't even count post-release therapies, both mental and physical, that were of much greater duration than the post-release therapy protocols for any other type of injury.

This is a very partial view of gun violence because it involves only instances where someone was actually shot with a gun. In fact, the latest figures show that roughly 85,000 people are either killed or wounded by firearms each year (of which 30,000 result in death), but nearly another 400,000 people are menaced, robbed, beaten up or otherwise victimized by someone with a gun.[2] And that's a minimal figure. David Hemenway, the noted gun scholar expert at Harvard's School of Public Health, estimates instances in which people are menaced or made to feel threatened by guns to be in the millions every year.

As we will see in the next chapter, the pro-gun lobby would like you to believe that this figure would be much higher were it not for the "fact" that so many law-abiding Americans go walking around each day carrying a gun, and act as a deterrent against even a higher level of gun crimes or gun violence or some form of unauthorized gun use. You'll have to think about that issue in detail when you read the chapter which follows, but in the meantime let's just say that the real number of Americans who experience gun violence as victims is certainly more than half a million, and if it's true, then that's a serious number. It really is.

Let's look at that number a little more closely. Start again with the number of people—85,000—that are killed or wounded with guns. According to the latest figures, approximately 35% of all American households possess at least one gun. As Bill Clinton would say, do the arithmetic: this means that roughly 70 million adults have access to guns, and that's a minimal number. Now let's divide that number by the 85,000 who are killed or maimed; the victims of gun violence as it's usually computed constitute .0012 percent of all the people who own guns. Sorry, but it's not a very impressive number, and it would never get any attention were it not for the fact that a tiny percentage of that tiny percentage are high-profile victims like the kids in Sandy Hook or Gabby Giffords, or John Lennon or Martin Luther King or JFK.

But if we add in the number of people who were menaced or threatened by a gun but didn't become a statistic in the *dead-wounded* category, all of a sudden we are dealing with more than 1% of all the people who own guns. And that's a much bigger number; actually 100 times larger than the ones who actually get shot. Now what's the reason why, like the veritable Chinese menu, we have so few people, dead and wounded, in Column A and so many people, menaced, in Column B? We don't know. In fact, we don't have one earthly idea. And yet we have study after study, the latest appearing in the *Annals of Internal Medicine* in January, 2014, which proves again and again that if a gun is lying around, the odds of a homicide and particularly a suicide go up.[3] But what about all those guns lying around that are used to intimidate, or create great fear, or get something accomplished without the trigger being pulled? Isn't that gun violence too? Of course it is, with the only difference being dumb, blind luck.

To talk about gun violence as only involving incidents in which a gun is actually fired is to miss the whole point of this book. Because we simply do not know when, why or how the line between not using a gun and using a gun is crossed by someone who is, as I referred to it earlier, thinking of using a gun in an unauthorized way or even isn't thinking about it but is in a position to do it. I would not have written this book just to tell you about the 85,000 Americans who get shot each year with a gun. I'm interested in them to be sure, but I'm even more interested in the hundreds of thousands who weren't shot but could have been shot if the trigger of the gun pointed in their direction had actually been pulled. And that's what I mean when I talk about the difference between violence and violence with guns.

In April, 2013, during the post-Sandy Hook gun debate, the Department of Justice issued a report which showed that levels of gun violence, particularly homicides committed with guns, was continuing to go down. Meanwhile, the same report showed that the total number of non-fatal crimes involving guns had actually increased by more than 25 percent over the three previous years, while gun homicides had declined during the same period by a whopping 8 percent. So if we define gun violence by homicide levels, the NRA was correct in making the argument that we have become much less violent without additional gun controls. If, on the other hand, you change the definition of gun violence to embrace every unauthorized use of a gun, then we have a much bigger problem than we had just a few years ago. And as I will explain further on, the moment a gun is pulled out for anything other than its authorized use, the odds that it won't go off come down to nothing but chance.

Which brings us to an issue I want to get out of the way in this book as early as possible, namely, the whole question of the data that is used to talk about gun violence. In a word, it's lousy. The data isn't quite as lousy as the arguments that are often fashioned by people and organizations using the data, but it's not very good. And it's not very good for two reasons. First, this is a very large country, and since data on gun crime and gun use is generated for the most part by laws or procedures that are used to control guns, the data reflects the division of authority between federal, state and local governments, all of whom keep their own records and none of whom necessarily share the information with anyone else. For example, take the question of gun crime, or crimes of violence in general. At the top of the pyramid is the FBI which is mandated by law to report on crime through the publication of the Uniform Crime Report, or as it is usually known, the UCR. The good news about the UCR is that, in general, the definitions of different types of crimes—homicide, assault, robbery, burglary, etc.—is pretty uniform throughout all 50 states. But some states set the minimum age for adult defendants at 18, others at 17, still others at 16 or even lower, depending on the type of crime. And this variation can lead to significant problems in comparing data from one state to another because the majority of all violent crimes in the United States are committed by males between the ages of 16 and 30. So if you move the minimum age up or down a year, you might miss a lot of crime.

The other problem with the UCR is that it is based on reporting from the states which is not required reporting, nor is it necessarily a requirement that a local law enforcement agency in a particular state report its numbers to a centralized state agency which then forwards those numbers to the FBI. And then within each state there's a further breakdown between different types of agencies—county, city, town and so forth—which makes any degree of uniform reporting at best a vague hope. In fact, the greatest irony is that the FBI refers to its data as the *uniform* crime report, when in fact there isn't very much about it that's uniform at all. Which doesn't mean the data is useless. To the contrary, the FBI makes a real effort to insure at least a degree of consistency in its reporting by trying to utilize information from the same agencies each year. They also make sure to collect enough data from each region so that the data is not only fairly representative but, if not exact as to numbers, at least represents a fairly valid trend.

Here's the bottom line when it comes to crime data: the good news is that most law enforcement agencies do a pretty good job of tracking crimes because it's the most important measure they can use to determine how they are doing their job and how much they should be paid. The bad news is that, the last time I looked, there were at least four different federal agencies issuing reports on crime and each one looks at the data in a slightly different way or uses it for different purposes. First we have the FBI and its Uniform Crime Reports, as well as its Supplemental Homicide Reports; then there's the DOJ's Bureau of Justice Statistics, which issues its own report on crime plus a second report on crime victims; and then there's the CDC which runs the National Violent Death Reporting System and the Web-Based Injury Statistics Query and Reporting System. You can assume that any time I use data in this book it came from one, or a combination of the sources listed above. I'm giving you these details because further on in the text I am going to use data from these sources to make some pretty provocative statements about gun violence and I want to make sure that you understand that I'm not inventing anything out of whole cloth. The data I'm using in this book is diffuse, sometimes incomplete and has to be used with caution. But nothing which follows in this narrative is invented or made up.

In all of the concern about data validity, there is one bright spot when we talk about the use of such data to understand gun violence: of all crime categories, the one for which the data is most reliable is homicide, due to the simple reason that it's hard not to notice a body when the body's lying in the street. And even if the body's sitting in a dumpster or sprawled on the floor of the back room of an abandoned house, sooner or later the smell's going to give it away. So we don't have the kind of reporting problems that tends to skew data that we have, for example, when we are talking about crimes like larceny and rape.

On the other hand, and there's always another hand when it comes to crime and crime data, we really have to be careful about what we know and what we don't know, even when we are talking about something as simple and obvious as toting up all the dead bodies which became dead in some unnatural way. In 2010, according to the FBI, there 14,748 homicides in the United States. According to the CDC, which ranks homicides as one of the 113 leading causes of morbidity, the correct number of homicides was 16,259. How could there be a difference of 10% between homicides reported by the FBI versus homicides reported by the CDC? Answer: Beats hell out of me.

Which brings us to the second big issue that has bedeviled crime researchers from virtually the first time that anyone began trying to analyze crime, namely, the question of reported versus unreported criminal events. The problem with relying on law enforcement agencies for crime data is that what you are really relying on is the decision by everyday citizens to report crimes to the police, which is not the same thing as a crime taking place. So when a particular type of crime increases or decreases, are we really looking at more or less crimes, or at the willingness or unwillingness of citizens to report crimes, or both?

Let's think about one category of crime, domestic violence, or what is commonly referred to as intimate partner violence or IPV. Actually, domestic violence isn't a separate category of violent crime, as is rape or aggravated assault. It may, in fact, fall into either of those categories, and it wasn't until the last ten years or so that women in particular felt encouraged to discuss or report it at all. So, for example, since 1993 all violent crime rates dropped by 48 percent according to the FBI, whereas rape dropped only by one-third. Is this differential perhaps a reflection of the under-reporting of rape before 1993? We simply do not know.

While one might think that statistical and analytical models could be employed to more precisely differentiate crime between reported and unreported numbers, a rather disquieting trend about the perception of criminal activity has recently emerged that throws into doubt our ability to distinguish between *committed* as opposed to *reported* criminal events. What I am referring to is the degree to which Americans seem to believe that serious crime is on the increase, even though the numbers may indicate otherwise. For example, in May 2013, Pew published a study borrowing FBI and DOJ data which showed a decade-long decline in violent gun crimes in excess of 50%. Meanwhile, in a national poll, more than 50% of respondents told Pew that they believed serious crime rates were going up.[4] The Gallup organization conducted a poll around the same time which found that a majority of Americans believed their own neighborhoods to be safer while, at the same time, they felt that the country overall was less safe. Could these perceptions just have been the result of Sandy Hook and the ensuing national debate, as some commentators surmised? We don't know.

Reporting a crime, any crime, forces the victim to weigh the consequences of contacting the police or not contacting the police. And this decision obviously involves considering one's previous experience with the police, as well as the willingness to use formal channels (police, courts, etc.) to redress the results of a criminal act. Because all these variables impact crime data drawn from law enforcement sources (never mind the frequent allegations that various police agencies "cook" crime numbers to satisfy various political agendas), researchers turn to another source for crime information: the medical system. Chief among medical agencies providing data is the CDC, which uses a system known as WISQARS, which stands for Web-based Injury Statistics Query and Reporting System, and NVDRS, which stands for the National Violent Death Reporting System. Both of these databases can be used in conjunction with the law enforcement data to create a fairly comprehensive, if not complete picture of violent crime. But, reader beware, in addition to not being complete, the data isn't current.

I make this last point because in the wake of Sandy Hook, a spate of web-based reporting sites have sprung up, such as Mother Jones and Slate, which purport to present real-time data on gun violence, except that it's not data in the traditional sense of the word at all. These sites derive their content from reports by readers who link to their local news sources, as well as from web crawlers and other search mechanisms that pick up digital mention of words like 'guns' or 'shootings' or 'violence' or what have you. The data is presented in graphic and arresting formats but it's notably incomplete. Here's a quick reality check for those of you who are obsessive enough (like me) to have followed my argument to this point: data on gun violence from sources that are legally required to report such information is, at best, eighteen to twenty-four months behind the current date. That's correct. Eighteen to twenty-four months.

One more brief caveat about data and then I'll move into the heart of the gun violence issue itself. Unfortunately, I probably wouldn't be writing this or my previous or subsequent volumes on guns had it not been for Sandy Hook. That one event created a firestorm of comments and publications that motivated me and others to share our thoughts and opinions about anything and everything having to do with guns. And historically, it has always been a horrific killing incident or a notable victim that provokes the debate. But statistically, even the killing of 26 people in Newtown doesn't change gun violence data very much. It changes the gun violence for Newtown of course, and for Connecticut, but not for the country as a whole.

Nor, as it turns out, after waiting nearly a year for the official report on Newtown from the State Attorney General, did we ever learn much about the motives or circumstances that led Adam Lanza to commit his indescribable murders. For that matter, Jared Loughner has yet to tell us anything about why he shot Gabby Giffords and others, even though more than two years have elapsed since he committed that brutal act. I am intending to cover mass shootings in a chapter of Volume 4 in this series, but I suspect I'll end up saying much the same about those events that I will end up saying about one-on-one gun violence events in this book.

Over the last several years, beginning around 2010, guns have killed roughly 30,000 people and wounded another 50,000 each year.[5] The total number has swung back and forth a bit, but we seem to have stabilized when guns go off in what I call unauthorized fashion and someone gets hit at about 80,000 times annually. I say 'stabilized' because from 1994 until 2001 the number was in a kind of free-fall, from a high of 121,000 in 1993 (18,000 homicides, 17,000 suicides, the remaining accidents and injuries/assaults) to around 75,000 in 2001 and then moving slightly back upwards over the last few years, due largely to a steady rise in gun suicides. These numbers are fairly consistent and, notwithstanding what I said earlier about the quality of data (or the lack of quality) we can reasonably assume that gun violence in the U.S., defining violence as a physical injury caused by a gun, claims roughly 80,000 people a year. Bloomberg's research group at Johns Hopkins would push the number above 100,000, so take your pick.[6] But either way, I do not believe that this gives us any realistic understanding of the dimensions of the problem. And worse, it doesn't shed any light on how to even define the problem.

Because if we are going to try and figure out what the term "gun violence" really means, first I think we need to spend a little time talking about violence, whether or not guns are involved. Someone who uses a gun to commit an act of violence has already decided to commit that act, or is capable of committing such an act before picking up the gun. In and of itself the weapon is of secondary importance because there are other weapons available and, in fact, more people are hit with clubs or stabbed with knives than shot with guns. The difference, as I indicated earlier, is that the gun is a very definitive way to commit violence, definitive because it is so efficient (all you have to do is aim it in the right direction) and the results are so destructive. We'll show you what we mean from a data perspective shortly. Right now I want to slow down a bit and talk about violence itself.

Ever hear of the NICHQ Vanderbilt Assessment Scale? It's a diagnostic tool used by physicians (and can also be used by parents) to determine whether a child has ADHD, otherwise known as Attention Deficit Hyperactivity Disorder. This condition affects roughly 8 percent of the population ages 3-17, or at least that's the percentage of this age cohort that has been diagnosed with this disorder. The Vanderbilt assessment consists of 40 questions, of which roughly half attempt to capture performance in a classroom environment, while the other half focus on the child's own behavior rather than his or her performance within a group. The child's behavior rating is based on how frequently they exhibit certain behavioral traits from "never" to "very often," and as the total score moves upwards, the ADHD diagnosis becomes more evident (although the medical academies are insistent on the use of Vanderbilt as one, but not the only diagnostic tool and procedure that must be utilized to confirm an ADHD condition in any child.)

Study after study has linked untreated ADHD to excessive and/or disruptive levels of anger which, in the most extreme cases, leads to violent behavior. And here are some of the behavioral traits which, if scored as 'often' or 'very often' on the Vanderbilt, point toward a diagnosis of ADHD:

- Bullies, threatens, or intimidates others

- Initiates physical fights

- Lies to obtain goods for favors or to avoid obligations (e.g. "cons" others)

- Is physically cruel to people

- Has stolen items of nontrivial value

- Deliberately destroys others' property

Notice how most of these behaviors involve actual physical violence. Notice as well how these behaviors involve not just violence, but the conscious use of violence to obtain something, to get something, to *achieve some desired result.* And this is the context in which we need to understand the violent behavior that may, at times, result in using a gun. Because what most of us believe to be violent behavior, and thus anti-social behavior, and thus behavior that is "abnormal" or "aberrant" when compared to "normal" social norms, may in fact not fit any of those categories at all when viewed from the perspective of the person committing the violence itself.

Bear in mind that virtually all of our data on violent behavior is drawn from data about crime;

number of crimes, type of crimes, number of victims, cost, etc. So we are assuming that violence is a negative event in the community which has harmful effects for each victim and the community as a whole. That's why we criminalize certain types of behavior, usually the most extreme and hurtful types, because we want it to occur as infrequently as possible.

But let's flip the coin over to the other side and begin with an anecdote mentioned by sociologist Peter Schneider, who tells that in an important meeting of top *mafiosi* in Sicily, one of the attendees arrived late and begged the group's forgiveness because, as he said, "I had to change a flat tire and I had to strangle Stefano Giaconia." His tardiness was excused because everyone agreed with him that the man he strangled had always been difficult and "given him trouble" right up to the end. In other words, how one evaluates violent behavior isn't just a function of normative criteria established by the whole society, it can also reflect the values, needs and behavioral goals of the social environment in which an act of violence takes place. Jacky Bouju, who has studied what he calls "ordinary social violence" in African cities, notes that violence from the perspective of the perpetrator may be a very rational and efficient way to obtain some desired effect or goal, and while it might also reflect a violation of certain social norms, it can be used to define or stress a personal identity that cannot otherwise be displayed or acknowledged to exist in the current social or cultural milieu.[7]

Don't get me wrong; I'm not trying to justify or romanticize violence. But also notice that this whole teeter-totter between violence and gun violence keeps slipping in, and therefore the existence or occurrence of violence may or may not have little if anything to do with the methods we use to analyze it, measure it, or control it. For example, much of the public policy debate about guns centers on a comparison of gun violence rates in the U.S. versus gun violence in other countries. It turns out that if you define violence in terms of serious crime, the U.S. is basically no less or no more violent than other Western countries. Researchers from the Injury Control Research Center at Harvard's School of Public Health have calculated that our rates of car theft, burglary, robbery, sexual assault and aggravated assault are similar to other high-income countries, but our violence is much more deadly; i.e., three times higher for adults, thirteen times higher for children ages 5 to 14.[8] They tie this difference to the existence of many more guns in the U.S. than in other advanced countries, which sounds logical and it's an argument accepted by most public policy advocates who believe in stricter control over firearm ownership and sales.

Unfortunately, the moment you try to correlate gun homicide rates with per-capita gun ownership, the argument begins to break down. For example, our per-capita gun ownership rate is 88 and Switzerland's rate is 45; in other words, about half. But our gun homicide rate per 100,000 is 3.6 and Switzerland's rate is .52, about one-sixth of our rate. Germany's ownership rate is 31, about one-third our rate; their gun homicide rate is .2, about one-twelfth our gun murder rate. If one basic fact emerges from a cross-country comparison between gun ownership and gun homicide, it's that there must be other factors that explain the difference between gun violence in America and gun violence everywhere else. I'm not arguing that there's no connection between our comparatively elevated gun violence level and the existence of two hundred to three hundred million guns. Nor am I attempting to cast doubt on the remarkable work conducted by David Hemenway and his colleagues at Harvard's School of Public Health. What I am saying, however, is that the assumption of a direct link between numbers of guns and numbers of gun deaths requires an explanation that goes further than what the comparison of data assumes it to be.

Which is why I want to go back to understanding the issue of violence before we even look at the question of guns. Because if our general violence level is no different from violence that occurs in other Western countries, could it be that the decision to escalate the violence to a higher level by pulling out a gun has to do with factors that lie outside the existence or the availability of the gun itself? This is where gun policy experts have focused their attention, but only when trying to figure out the reasons why people *stop* using guns. I am referring here to the arguments advanced to explain the nearly 50 percent decline in gun violence, particularly homicides, that took place between 1994 and 2001. During these seven years, gun homicide rates dropped significantly in almost every locality within the United States, as did rates of non-fatal gun violence, as did rates of violent crime as well. I discussed in detail the various explanations for these remarkable and unprecedented trends in *Guns for Good Guys, Guns for Bad Guys,* so I'll just briefly summarize them here (and then you can go buy the other book).

Three explanations seem to have some real currency: (1) The slowing down of the crack epidemic which had accounted for much of the very rapid crime and violence increase from the mid-80's until 1993; (2) the addition of more than 60,000 uniformed police officers as a result of the Clinton crime bill of 1994; (3) stricter and lengthier prison sentences increased the incarcerated population by more than one-half million and therefore kept many serious criminals off the streets.[9] There were also some loony ideas such as the elimination of leaded paint which contributed to a decline in ADHD; and the expansion of legal abortions following Rowe vs. Wade which meant that less unwanted (hence, unloved and worse-behaved) children were coming of age.

Chances are the decline in crime and violence between 1993 and 2001 can be explained through a combination of social, economic, demographic and political factors, because nothing as complicated as crime and violence can ever be explained through a simple "magic bullet" formula. But that's fine when we're talking about this brief period of quick decline; what about the nearly decade and a half since, when levels of violence and gun violence have remained more or less stable, if not actually begun to creep back up? If the answer is the existence of all those guns, then the rates of violence and gun violence should be sky-high because, according to the ATF, we've probably added at least one-third more guns to the public arsenal since 2001. But what is remarkable about violence and guns in the last few years is that the rates have moved a bit here and there, but have not significantly gone up or down at all. Could it be that for reasons I have not yet discussed, the United

States has a permanent level of violence and gun violence which might be impermeable to any real strategy for change? Or are there other reasons for this stability of violent behavior that has now lasted more than ten years?

Let's start with some basic data that at least gives us a profile of gun violence in terms of where it occurs, why it occurs and who's involved in its occurrence. Here's the where, starting at the state level:[10] a map in which the states are shaded by gun homicide rates, the gray states being right around the national average of 3.2 gun homicides per 100,000 residents, darker states above the average and lighter states below it:

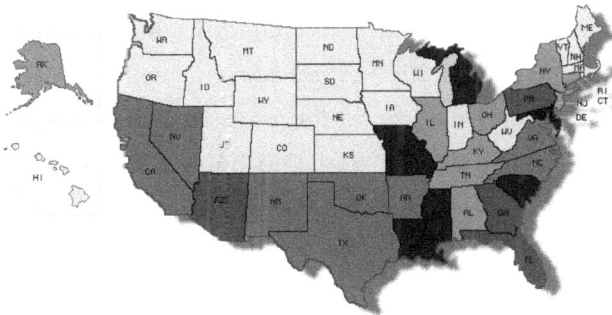

Map 1 – Gun homicide rate by state

In 2010 the lightest states on this map contained 62 million residents, exactly one-fifth of the total American population. These 22 states, of whom 12 had more gun owners per capita than the national average, had a gun homicide rate of 1.3 per 100,000 residents, not as low as the EEU countries, but a far cry from our overall number. Does this mean there's no link between gun violence and the extraordinary number of guns that are floating around? That seems to be the case in the western half of the country. But the point of the map is to force us to exercise some caution in painting the gun violence picture with strokes that might be too broad to do anything more than obscure the real questions that need to be asked.

For example, now that we know where gun violence occurs, at least at the state level, does the significantly lower gun homicide rates in the lightest states correlate with other data that might tell us more about how and why gun violence occurs? Here's something to consider: overall, guns were used in 67 percent of all 2010 homicides, a fairly consistent figure from one year to the next. But in the 22 states that registered the lowest gun homicide rates, only 3 states registered 67 percent gun use in homicides, with the rest coming in at between 16 percent for Hawaii and in the 40 and 50 percent range for most of the Western and Plains states. In other words, as gun homicide rates decline relative to overall homicide rates, so does the use of guns to commit homicides.

Why is this important? If you haven't figured it out yet, I'll break it to you gently: while this is a book about gun violence, it's mostly a book about the people who commit gun violence. And that's because almost all of the studies of gun violence focus not on the people who commit violence with a gun, but on the people who become the victims of that particular type of violent act. This isn't because we are biased to think more about the victim than the perpetrator, although that might be the case. It's because most of the available data points us in the direction of the victim. So let's begin by considering the data. Where does it come from? For the most part it derives from a penal system that was actually developed more than a thousand years ago and was, as it first appeared and used, the basis of all legal codes and legal authority in the Western world.

Today we think about law as being civil law on the one hand and criminal law on the other. And it is civil law, the law that enforces contracts and property rights, which is considered the more important and (certainly for the legal profession) the more lucrative form of legal activity in which to be involved. Yet historically, criminal codes were the first published legal codes and were used by early monarchs and other political leaders to assert their political authority and sovereignty over the community as a whole. The reason for this was because it was recognized, as early as the fourth or fifth century, and perhaps even earlier, that without some formal system to adjudicate physical disputes, the human community might easily crumble in the face of incessant feud. So mechanisms had to be developed to make sure that if one person suffered an injury at the hands of another, that he could be compensated for his loss in a manner that would mitigate what otherwise would be some sort of behavior motivated by the desire for revenge.

It was the notion of physical or economic injury, of someone losing something of value at the hands of another, even if what he lost was his life, that created the first legal systems and penal definitions which are still in force today. Terms like "robbery," or "murder" or "assault" were being used in courtrooms throughout Europe and England in the early Middle Ages, and the definitions that were attached to such words in the 5th or 6th centuries were no different than the definitions we find in current federal and state compendiums of criminal procedures and laws.

To better understand my perspective, take a quick look at the FBI's Uniform Crime Reports that are issued each year and present a very detailed picture of criminal activity throughout the United States. The reports are compiled on the basis of different criminal activities—crime categories such as murder, assault, robbery, burglary and so forth. The report breaks down these crimes by geography and by all sorts of demographic information about the victim. In the case of gun homicides, for example, we can quickly figure out where the shootings took place and who was shot (age, sex, race, etc.), but our ability to figure out the same information *about the shooter* is much less clear.

Part of the bias towards data based on the victim is due to the unfortunate fact that the moment a crime is reported, we have an event that can be categorized in many different ways: type, location, demographics of the victim, etc. So, by definition, there will be some kind of information available for analysis of 100 percent of all crimes, if only if the crime itself is defined. In 2012 the FBI registered 6,050,000 victims of violent crime of all kinds. But the same data-set only counts 4,556,000 "known offenders," which does not refer to the actual identify of the perpetrator, but simply that one physical attribute (gender, for example) was known or at least reported to be known. If you get bopped over the head and tell the police that the person who bopped you was a male, the FBI picks that up as a "known" offender, even though what you said won't go very far to help make an arrest. Furthermore, although roughly 46% of violent crimes against persons resulted in an arrest, tracking ultimate convictions back to that arrest and further back to a specific crime is a difficult, if not impossible task. Comparing number of violent felonies to convictions in about a dozen states results in an annual conviction rate of about 50 percent. But were those convictions for crimes committed the same year? Who the hell knows?

I know you're getting glassy-eyed reading about how to deal with the endless statistics and I'm getting just as glassy-eyed writing about it. So I'm going to stop here and try to sum up a bit: We are going to have to get very, very specific in order to really understand or even define the issue of gun violence, particularly from the perspective of the shooter rather than the victim. The numbers that are collected by local, state and federal law enforcement agencies don't really match up. In Chapter 3 I'll come back to the numbers but at the street-corner level which may tell us about the overall situation or they may not.

Let's begin talking about who uses guns by figuring out the extent of the problem from a behavioral point of view, or what I referred to earlier as the *unauthorized* use of a gun. In 2010 there were 310 million people living in the United States, a number that has probably increased to nearly 318 million at the time (February, 2014) I'm writing this text. By the end of this year probably around 1.4 million people will have committed violent crimes, i.e., murder, rape, robbery and aggravated assault. This number takes into account the fact that some people commit more than one crime and, at the same time, reported crimes are always somewhat lower than the actual numbers of crimes.

Out of this total, roughly 400,000 of these individuals will use or at least carry a gun during the commission of the crime. Out of that number, somewhere between 40,000 and 50,000 (or perhaps even higher) will pull the trigger, and the only reason that only a quarter of the uses of the gun will result in a homicide is because the other three-quarters of the gun users aren't good shots. The problem is that even though data from the FBI's Uniform Crime Report (UCR), the Justice Department's National Crime Victimization Survey (NCVS) and the CDC's Web-based Injury Statistics Query and Reporting System (WISQUARS) allows us to estimate the number of crime gun victimizations at 400,000, this doesn't mean that we can use the same number to estimate how many people, with the possible intention of committing some kind of violence, are walking around with a gun.

Now the one thing we do know about this entire typology, from walking around with a gun to actually using it, the one thing we can say with absolute, scientific certainty, is that nobody comes out of the womb with a gun in their hand. So at some point everyone who ends up in the category of human beings from whom at least 400,000 actually use a gun in a violent act, made the conscious decision to acquire a gun and, at some later point in time, to use it in an unauthorized; i.e., violent way. Thus, if we are going to figure out who these people are who commit gun violence, as opposed to figuring out who the people are who become victims of gun violence, we have to start at the point when a conscious decision was made by each and every one of them to get their hands on a gun: when, how and why.

As you might suspect, the data that covers these issues is diffuse and difficult in many cases to understand. But let's give it a try. The fundamental research on when and how guns were acquired was published by Daniel Webster and other researchers associated with Mike Bloomberg's gun violence think tank at Johns Hopkins in 2002.[11] The research team studied 45 "criminally involved" youths who were incarcerated in a juvenile detention facility and were between the ages of 14 and 18, an age cohort in which inner-city gun use is significantly high. What they learned was that the pattern that most kids followed in acquiring guns was no different from what young people do in buying cars; start with something used and cheap, followed by newer and more expensive models. Most of the kids in this study admitted to spending less than $100 for a small, cheaply made used pistol in 22, 25 or 32 caliber, and then in most cases graduated to newer, larger, more powerful and more expensive guns in calibers like 357, 9mm or 45.

What is interesting about this study is it turns out that the illegal or "underground" gun market operates the same way and with the same flow and cost of products as the legal market. The fact that virtually none of these kids could qualify to purchase a handgun legally, if for no other reason than handgun ownership in Maryland is prohibited for anyone under the age of 21, didn't stop them from behaving in exactly the way that most people behave who purchase guns legally from the local gun shop of their choice. Most of the kids also reported that they had owned multiple guns with the average slightly more than 3 guns for each respondent in the study and one youth admitting to the ownership of 11 firearms. In this respect, the behavior of criminally linked youth was no different than the behavior of legal gun owners, almost all of whom, as hobbyists, possess multiple guns.

The one issue that the study did not cover, however, was to determine the motivation for gun ownership in the first place. This information is available in a study published by Professor Alan Lizotte and colleagues in 2000, based on interviews with more than 600 young men in Rochester, New York, that covered a six-year period during which time the average age for all the respondents was 14, increasing to 20 over the period of the study.[12] In the earlier years, youths reported acquiring guns as a function of membership in gangs for reasons of self-protection and/or peer pressure. As study respondents aged, the decision to carry a gun was based on the necessity to protect oneself in the course of dealing drugs, a behavior that was considered a logical response to the business environment in which they operated. At both stages of the cycle, respondents who did not belong to gangs and who later did not sell drugs reported much fewer instances in which they carried weapons.

The data on when and why guns first start to be carried is confirmed by the Department of Justice graph (below) that shows participation in crimes by age cohort, with property crimes increasing dramatically after 12 years, peaking at 16 years and immediately tumbling back down by age 22, whereas violent crime increases much more gradually beginning at age 14, peaking at age 18 but then slowly receding yet remaining significant until the mid-30's. The fact that kids reported acquiring a small, cheap gun in their early teens but then "trading up" to a higher-caliber, newer model with more "business" potential, underscores the degree to which patterns of crime participation change from lesser to more violent crime activities as kids move up the age scale and become adults.

United States

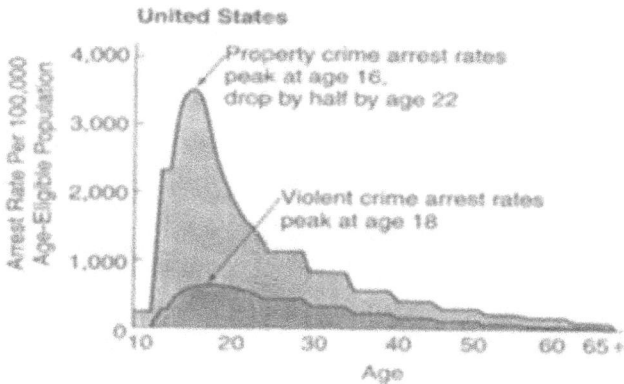

So this answers the questions of "why" and "when" guns first appear in the population which uses them to commit violence, but it doesn't answer the bigger question as to why the violence is committed at all. Because even though as much as half the acts of juvenile violence are never reported to the authorities, hence the UCR numbers on juvenile crime may be seriously underestimated, the fact is that the overwhelming majority of children who are located even in neighborhoods and environments that experience inflated levels of violence go through their juvenile or adolescent life-spans without being involved in violent behavior. Or certainly not the kind of violent behavior that propels them forward into continuous and serious acts of violent crime.

And this is an important distinction to be made for two reasons. First, because violent behavior that ultimately manifests itself in violent criminal acts does not often appear out of nowhere, at least not from a chronological point of view. The precedents for this behavior occur as early as pre-adolescent childhood, usually taking the form of observing violent behavior in the home. By the time children from such dysfunctional families enter school, in many instances they begin almost immediately to exhibit anti-social behavior that will become more violent as they get older.

The second reason why the early onset of violent behavior is important to understand is that it also clearly influences the choice of peer groups and peer-group activity which leads to violence and then to committing violent crimes. Children begin to make conscious choices about social contacts at an early age, and the degree to which parents and other adults can guide such decisions decreases as kids enter their teenage years. Much research has affirmed the fact that gang membership is not unusual in the early adolescent years, and in neighborhoods where gangs are present, they tend to attract the kids whose predisposition to anti-social behavior will be tolerated, if not genuinely encouraged by the ethos of the gang. Almost all of the adolescents in Lizotte's study who reported owning guns also reported being members of gangs, and while they often "graduated" to serious criminal activities (and ownership of better guns) at the time that active gang enrollment ceased, the link between serious crime and gun ownership had already been set.

If nothing else, the discussion of the last several pages at least yields some important clues as to why and when young boys begin to carry guns. But this still doesn't tell us about the what and the who; we still need to figure out who was the object of the violent behavior that involved the use of a gun, and what actually happened that: a) brought the gun into plain view, and, b) resulted in the trigger being pulled. Because we can't assume that everyone walking around with an unauthorized gun is necessarily going to pull it out every time that a possible violent act is about to occur. And even if that's true, we certainly know from the numbers that, at best, for every time that a trigger was pulled, the gun itself had been brandished or used in some way without being shot at least ten times.

Unfortunately we cannot locate data that illustrates the relationship of attacker to victim for all felonies with the exception of homicide. But homicide may be the most decisive criminal category for figuring out the use of guns in violence because in cases of murder, guns are used to such a frequent degree. Guns are the weapon of choice in both aggravated assaults and robberies roughly 30 percent of the time, but they are used in felony murders more than two-thirds and perhaps as often as three-quarters of the time. In other words, when someone wants to commit a robbery or a serious assault, the victim is only going to be facing a gun in a minority of instances. But if the trigger is pulled, the odds go up considerably that the crime will end up with a dead body on the floor.

On the other hand, we have pretty good data on the types of crimes that resulted in someone ending up dead, data which is probably fairly representative for non-homicide gun violence as well. Because as I have discussed, most instances of gun homicide are escalations of confrontations that may or may not have been initiated with the display of a gun, but then sooner or later out it came. And this data, illustrated below, needs to be considered in very specific and detailed terms:

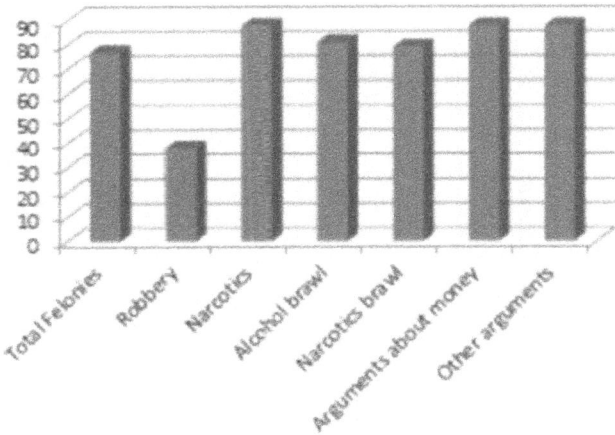

The above chart comes from the UCR for 2012, so it's pretty current stuff. And what it illustrates is the percentage of felonies in different categories in which the killer and the victim had some degree of personal relationship before the homicidal event actually took place. This illustration is based on what may be the single most important dataset that I will utilize in this entire book, so I'm going to treat this information very carefully, thoroughly and specifically.

What is represented above is the percentage of total homicides, as well as the specific circumstances of homicides in which the two individuals knew each other. Overall, a personal relationship between attacker and victim existed in slightly more than 70 percent of all events. But with the exception of robberies, the personal nature of homicides registered for the most part above 80 percent. Now follow closely.

The above chart covers 5,451 homicides out of an overall total of 12,765. Of the overall number, police reports did not specify relationships between attacker and victim in 55 percent of the murders, but there's no reason to assume that if every report had been completely filled out that the results would have differed from what we see above because a sample of 42 percent out of nearly 13,000 events is certainly representative in anyone's book.

It's even more representative for overall homicide when we consider not just the percentage of homicides in which attacker and victim were in some way connected, but the actual distribution of connected homicides based on the circumstances of the crime. Of the 5,451 homicides covered by the above graph, 2,400 occurred during arguments. With the exception of robberies, there was no other circumstantial category captured in the above chart that represented even a fraction of that total. And while less than 40 percent of all robberies that ended in a homicide involved a personal relationship between attacker and victim, the total of all robberies that produced a dead body was only 5 percent of all homicides reported to the FBI. In other words, people who robbed other people were largely intent on getting away with what they robbed. People who got into arguments, on the other hand, ended up in circumstances which, more often than not, resulted in an end to someone's life.

Finally, the last piece of this homicide data that we need to discuss covers the specific relationship of the victim to the perpetrator. The FBI lists nine specific family relationships (mother, father, sister, etc.) and eight non-family relationships, including girlfriend, acquaintance, neighbor, employer and so forth. While domestic violence as an aspect of overall violence has received a significant amount of attention in recent years, the homicide data is somewhat ambiguous because although more than 1,100 women were murdered in 2012, this number may, in fact, be more than 1,600. This is because, as stated earlier, less than half of the homicide reports did not go into gender or other detail in terms of the identity of the victim.

On the other hand, if the number of women who were murdered in 2012 might be twice as high as reported by the FBI, the same would probably hold true for the largest relational homicide category, namely acquaintances. Of the total homicides for which relational data was furnished, roughly 75% of the victims knew their attackers, either because they were members of the same family (22%) or were friends or acquaintances (57%). In total, 1,500 victims, or 22%, were believed to have had no personal relationship, family or otherwise, to the person who murdered them. While the relationship or non-relationship between victim and attacker was only known in slightly more than half of all homicides committed in 2012, the sample is large enough to state with a great degree of confidence that if someone walked up to you, stuck a gun in your face and pulled the trigger, the chances were 4 out of 5 that you knew this person before he or she made the decision to end your life.

One more caveat that needs to be explicitly mentioned and understood: some of the data used in this chapter covers homicide in general, while others covers homicides committed with a gun. Since at this point in the narrative I'm trying to establish some basic generalities on which I will later hang some more specific arguments, I feel confident using both types of data in talking about guns. Why? Because guns aren't used in two-thirds of all homicides in the United States, which is the number usually bandied about in virtually every study in the field. That figure is too low. In fact, guns are probably used in more than 75-80 percent of all homicides, which means that if we plug in data on homicides per se, rather than on homicides specifically tied to guns, the data for both categories will usually lead us to the same place.

The reason that most gun scholarship understates the existence of guns in American homicide is because the understatement begins at the incident point of the homicide itself. Last year (2012) there were 12,000+ homicides, of which 8,500 were committed with guns. This is the figure from the BJS (Bureau of Justice Statistics) and it's accepted by everyone this side of the moon. But if you take the trouble to look at the raw data which is used to derive these numbers (FBI-UCR) you quickly discover that for more than 15% of all homicides, no weapon or method is stated at all. And this is not the same thing as saying that the weapon was "undetermined." There is a specific category, if you want a checkbox, for homicides in which the investigators couldn't figure out exactly how the guy (or girl) was killed. No, I'm talking about the actual reports that, in the aggregate, constitute the UCR.

So here's what happens. We know the total number of homicides, so we always, more or less, can come up with a pretty accurate body count. But there are lots of times that the corpse is discovered just when the shift's about to change, the gun's going to wind up being melted down anyway and the chances of actually closing the case in an urban neighborhood are probably less than 25 percent, so the body goes to the morgue, the gun goes in an evidence locker back to the station and who really cares? It doesn't take a rocket scientist to figure out that if guns were the homicide method in two-thirds of the 75% of homicides where the method is actually described, then the chances are that guns will be two-thirds of the way in which people were killed in the reports where right now no method or mechanism is described. But if we take the 12,000-plus homicides and divide them by this new number, we wouldn't be dividing 12,000+ homicides by 7,000 guns, we'd be dividing 12,000+ homicides by somewhere around 9,000 guns. And that's no longer two-thirds. That's going on four-fifths.

The purpose of this chapter was to come up with a way to define gun violence. I'm not sure we have done that, but at least we now know, in general terms, where and against whom it takes place. To sum it up, the odds are that if you are the victim of an act of gun violence, you got into an argument with someone who had a gun, and you knew that person before the argument began. To put it another way, if we counted up every gun homicide that fit this profile and deducted them from the total gun homicides each year, the issue wouldn't ever make the evening news even if someone important got shot. And the only reason for some difference in homicide and assault profiles is that, as I have said previously, in some states they're not such great shots.

In the next chapter I'm going to talk about the when, and by that I mean the distinction between using gun violence for an authorized reason as opposed to using it in an unauthorized event. But before we end this chapter, let me remind you again about one simple thing: there isn't a single other consumer product freely or not so freely available that can do what guns can do. Sure, there are plenty of other weapons around—knives, clubs, chains—that can inflict serious damage if they bounce off or stick through human flesh. But you don't need to come up right next to someone to hit them with a gun. And you don't need to be even a fraction of their size to put them away for good. Remember the old Charles Atlas ads? The ones that featured the 97-pound weakling who was bullied all over the beach until he purchased an Atlas barbell set and added those great-looking biceps to his frame?

The problem with following the Atlas approach is that it might take month, if not years to change yourself into someone whose physique would scare off any other guy from walking up and slapping you in the face. But I'll bet those barbells cost just as much, if not more in 1950, than what you'd pay for a 9mm pistol today. Want to make sure that nobody's going to *diss* you in front of that pretty girl who just smiled as she walked by? It's simple: don't be the last guy on the block, to be caught without your Glock.

Notes to Chapter 1

1. Craig Newgard, et. al., "Gunshot Injuries in Children Served by Emergency Services," Pediatrics, online edn., October 14, 2013.

2. Death and injury data from various publications of the Bureau of Justice Statistics including the National Crime Victimization Survey, FBI-UCR publications, including Supplementary Homicide Reports and CDC Morbidity Reports and Annual Summaries. I refer to these publications throughout the narrative. All the gun-related publications of every agency can be accessed on the agency's website.

3. On homicide and gun access, cf., Michael Siegel, et. al., "The Relationship Between Gun Ownership and Firearm Homicide Rates in the United States, 1981-2010," American Journal of Public Health, online edn., September 12, 2013. On suicide and gun access, cf., A. Anglemyer, et. al., "The Accessibility of Firearms and Risk for Suicide and Homicide Victimization Among Household Members, A Systematic Review and Meta-Analysis, " Annals of Internal Medicine, online edn., January 21, 2014.

4. Pew Research Center, "Gun Homicide Rate Down 49% Since 1993 Peak; Public Unaware," May 7, 2013. The Gallup poll can be found on the Gallup website.

5. Cf., Bureau of Justice Statistics, "Firearm Violence, 1993-2011," May 2013.

6. Daniel W. Webster and Jon S. Vernick, eds., Reducing Gun Violence in America (Baltimore, 2013), p. xxv.

7. Peter Schneider, "The cultural production of violence among Mafioso," and Jacky Bouju, "Ordinary daily social violence in Africa: an offspring of urban anomy and normative confusion," EASA08: Experiencing Diversity and Mutuality. Conference abstracts.

8. E. Richardson & D. Hemenway, "Homicide, Suicide, and Unintentional Firearm Fatality: Comparing the United States With Other High-Income Countries, 2003," The Journal of Trauma, 70, 1 (January, 2011), 238-243.

9. The crime decline theories are summarized and reviewed by Stene Levitt, "Understanding Why Crime Fell in the 1990s: Four Factors that Explain the Decline and Six that Do Not," Journal of Economic Perspectives, 18, 1 (Winter, 2004) 163-190.

10. Population data from the Census; crime data from the UCR.

11. Daniel W. Webster, et. al., "How Delinquent Youths Acquire Guns: Initial Versus Most Recent Gun Acquiitions," Journal of Urban Health, 79, 1 (March, 2002), 60-69.

12. Alan J. Lizotte, "Factors Influencing Gun Carrying Among Young Urban Males Over The Adolescent-Young Adult Life Course," Criminology, 38, 3 (2000), 811-834.

CHAPTER 2

DO GUNS PROTECT US FROM GUNS?

NRA Advertisement - 1982

NRA Advertisement - 2013

When an African-American attorney from Texas began running YouTube videos promoting the idea that blacks, more than anyone, should be walking around with guns, I first thought this was an attempt by an anti-NRA group to ridicule the gun organization's vociferous campaign to promote concealed-carry licenses. Then I realized that Colion's video persona had become part and parcel of the NRA's public stance when his name and commentaries began appearing on NRA websites in March, 2013. This was the same time that a new extension of federal gun control was being debated in DC and it looked, to all intents and purposes, that something was actually going to take place. So the NRA was pulling out all its stops, including sending daily emails all over the place and ramping up its media campaign, in particular online videos, which accounted for the steady appearances of Colion Noir, whose real last name is Collins, and who became an instant sensation because here was a hip, cool, black dude telling everyone that they needed to carry a gun.

Colion, or Collins, or Noir, or whomever he really is was immediately denounced by all the usual gun control African-American liberal advocates, starting with Al Sharpton on down. And Noir's response, in part, was to claim that the government had been against Black gun ownership in the decades following the Civil War, which was all the more reason for modern-day black citizens to view contemporary gun control as just another way to keep minorities from having the same rights as enjoyed by everyone else. Further, he defended the NRA in particular because they had come out in favor of African Americans arming themselves when the Black Panthers began walking around Oakland carrying guns in open view. The only problem, of course, is that what he was saying in this respect simply wasn't true. But why let facts get in the way of opinions, right? After all, the NRA wasn't trying to influence public opinion. They were marketing their product and blacks were an underserved market as far as they were concerned.

The NRA has never gone out of its way, either way, to attract or repel minority membership, and there's no reason why they should. It's all about owning a gun, remember? And the fact that most NRA members are white men who live in the South doesn't make the organization in any way anti-black or anti-anyone else. On the other hand, it was the confrontations between the Panthers and the police in Los Angeles and other inner cities, set within the context of urban riots before and after 1968, that created the generalized feeling that American cities weren't safe. And when Charlton Heston began running a television ad for the NRA which pictured him walking down a darkened street in DC and referring to the city as the "murder capital of the world," you would have to be deaf, dumb and blind not to figure out that arguments about gun control were beginning to turn on the issue of race. In the interests of full disclosure, by the way, it should be added that the disarmament of former slaves by the "government," which Colion refers to in video after video, was in fact the handiwork of Jim Crow state governments in the South, not the liberal, federal government up North, an argument, by the way, that both Colion and Rand Paul seem to have gotten backwards. But if you're not going to let facts stand in the way of opinions, you're certainly not going to let them stand in the way of a good marketing campaign, that's for sure.

The fact that Colion Noir and his NRA sponsors want to play a little loose with history is not really of concern. What's more significant is the degree to which the NRA is marketing a new definition of gun ownership which can be best understood if one compares the two ads above, the first from 1982 and the second from 2012. The 1982 advertisement was in keeping with the NRA's long tradition of promoting hunting and sport shooting as clean, wholesome family fun. The promotion of Colion and his views on concealed carry, on the other hand, have nothing to do with family fun at all. The world has become a much scarier place, and this has led to a very clear change in the NRA's definition of how and why Americans should own guns. And the reason they say Americans—all Americans—should own guns is to protect themselves against criminals and crime. Which brings us to consider the question which forms the title of this chapter, namely, do guns protect their owners or anyone else from danger and from crime? Last chapter we dealt with the *what* of gun violence and now we are going to look at the *when*, as in when should you go around with a gun. Like it or not, the moment the gun goes off, some kind of violence—authorized or unauthorized—has taken place, and that's what this book is all about.

Actually, one of the first public figures to come out after Sandy Hook in advocating gun ownership and gun use for personal protection was none other than Vice President Joe Biden, who, after the President and perhaps Dianne Feinstein, is probably the most reviled politician by the pro-gun camp. In an interview in February, 2013, when the battle over a new federal gun control bill was in full tilt, Biden claimed that he told his wife Jill, "if there's ever a problem, just walk out on the balcony, take that double-barrel shotgun and fire two blasts outside the house." Biden was jumped on like crazy by the pro-gun gang for advocating the "indiscriminate" firing of a gun. And to show you how far removed from reality the gun argument has become, here was the very first time that an elected official from the Democratic side of the aisle and a staunch supporter of gun control had actually come out and explicitly endorsed the idea of using a gun, any gun, for self-defense, and all he got for his trouble was endless denunciations from the gun lobby because he was advocating the "unsafe" use of a gun. As if aiming a barrel filled with shot-shell in the air was unsafe; duhhh, ever go duck hunting?

When I read Biden's comment I was tempted to call Mossberg or Remington and tell them to immediately ship one of their shotguns to the Vice President's office so that he could take it home and give it to Jill. But nobody on the pro-gun side could ever think so creatively; rather, they had Colion Noir, the 29-year old gun expert from nowhere, come out with his first NRA-endorsed video in which he referred to Biden as "Elmer Fudd" who didn't know anything about modern gun technologies and who, into the bargain, had no right to be telling gun owners anything about how to defend themselves with guns.

It was when I saw this video, incidentally, that I realized that Colion Noir had stopped being a cute, funny and hip young man and had been turned into just another dopey NRA flack. Because the truth is that the inability of the NRA to step across the line and understand the value of Biden's comments reflected the fact that the organization was never interested in conducting a serious conversation about guns with people who didn't necessarily like guns; instead their strategy was and is to try and convince everyone that they should like guns because a gun is simply a device to protect yourself against crime. Which covers the *what* issue about guns, so now it's time to delve into some data to see if the addition of a gun to your basic list of carry-around items really will make you safer or not.

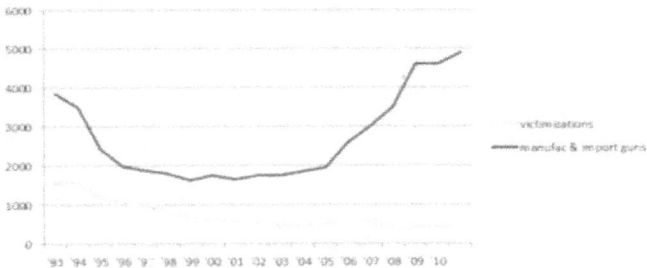

Let's begin the discussion with some very simple numbers. The above chart shows yearly totals of the number (in thousands) of handguns brought to the U.S. market through domestic manufacture and imports (in red) and the total gun victimizations (in thousands and in blue) courtesy of the ATF and BJS, respectively. The chart covers the years 1993 to 2011, a period when gun homicides and every category of violent crime dropped by more than 50 percent, although most of the decline occurred between 1993 and 2001. I could stuff this chapter full of more data, charts and graphs but this is the one piece of evidence that is always trotted out to justify the notion that more guns equals less crime.

Do yourself and me a favor, by the way, and don't try to nit-pick the data to death. I know its limitations and discrepancies better than you, believe me I do. But no matter how you slice it or dice it, the simple facts are that we have added somewhere around 60 million handguns to the civilian gun stash since 1993 and these guns, along with the rest of the civilian arsenal, are responsible for around 11,000 homicides each year over the last few years, a figure which in the early 90s appeared to be going to almost twice that number but, after 1993, the trend abruptly changed.

When it comes to arguments about how guns protect us from crime, the NRA has two gurus, Gary Kleck and John Lott. I dealt with Kleck at some length in *Guns for Good Guys, Guns for Bad Guys,* so I'll only deal with him briefly here. But let's hold off on him for a few pages and instead spend some time on Lott.[1] His book, *More Guns, Less Crime,* was an argument that set out to prove, exactly like his title, that personally owned guns were a deterrent to crime. The book first appeared in 1998, and was basically a response to CDC-funded studies that argued exactly the opposite, namely, that the existence of guns increased risk, particularly the risk of homicide or serious gun injury. Lott's initial edition ran into a shit-storm of criticism largely because it was suspected that, to be polite, the data on which it was based really didn't exist.

Over the intervening years Lott has become on the one hand a darling of the NRA and its media supporters (Fox News, The Washington Times, etc.) and anathema, on the other, to most academic scholars. Leaving aside the ins and outs of the validity of his data and/or methodology, Lott's basic argument boils down to the idea that in virtually every locality that he studied, he found a very strong correlation between the issuance of concealed carry gun permits and a decline in violent crime. His basic thesis stems from interviews with incarcerated felons, a majority of whom claimed that "they would not attack a potential victim who was known to be armed." Which sounds kind of obvious, when you stop and think about it, doesn't it? And despite the plethora of data and analysis which rolls off every page of Lott's book, the argument he's making is, in fact, pretty obvious and has become a watchword of the NRA's response to calls for more gun control. To quote Wayne LaPierre one week after Sandy Hook: "The only thing that stops a bad guy with a gun is a good guy with a gun."

Lott's book, which has now appeared in two updated editions, has become the selling point for expanded concealed carry arguments by gun groups, whether the argument is for less restrictions on ownership, or concealed carry, or for bringing guns into what have traditionally been gun-free zones, such as schools. And while I will shortly question both some of his data and his methodology, there is no doubt that the popularity of the book and its viewpoint on the relationship of guns to crime has paralleled a sweeping increase in legalizing concealed carry all over the United States.

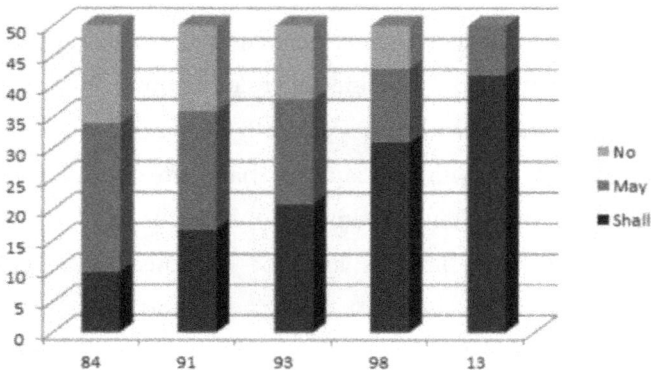

The above graph, beginning in 1984 and ending in 2013, distinguishes states by the type of concealed carry permit requirements that must be met by residents who want to walk around with a gun. The top portion of each column represents the number of states that did not grant any concealed carry permits, which ended when Illinois passed a CCW law in 2013. The middle portion of the columns, which have dropped from 24 states to 8 states (all of which with the exception of California are located in the Northeast) represent states that issue CCW permits but on a "discretionary" basis; i.e., the applicant must prove "need" for the carry privilege, in addition to meeting legal requirements. The bottom portion of the columns represent the number of states, 42 in 2013, whose laws generally grant CCW permits without requiring the applicant to meet any specific requirements other than the standard background check.

Here is where the evidence presented by Lott begins to break down. Because if you compare the gun victimization trends from the graph back on Page 41 to the increase in states granting concealed carry permits (see graph above), it immediately becomes clear that the great decline in violent crime took place between 1993 and 1998, whereas the spread of CCW permits happened in more states *after* 1998. I wouldn't attach such importance to the coincidence of these trends and certainly not assume that one trend necessarily tells us anything about the other, were it not for the fact that Lott's entire argument is based on assuming that the coincidence of falling crime levels and increasing concealed carry licensing has some kind of explanatory connection.

The real problem with his approach is that he uses selective data—crime levels and extension of CCW permits at the county level—when in fact the same decline in serious crime occurred at the same time in other jurisdictions where concealed carry permits were not yet allowed. How does he explain, for example, the fact that violent crime in the five counties that constitute New York City declined as quick, or quicker than violent crime in other jurisdictions, even though New York City's concealed carry permit system had not changed in any way since it was established on a very restricted basis in 1908?[2] He doesn't explain it and he doesn't even talk about it. If Lott believes that a correlation exists between more guns being carried around and less crime, it also becomes a problematic argument given what has happened since 2008, with the veritable explosion of gun sales following the election of Obama, the spread of CCW privileges to all 50 states and a miniscule decline in violent crime, and perhaps no decline in certain categories (aggravated assault, for example) at all. The years since 2008 mark the first time that the

American civilian gun market absorbed more than 4 million handguns in consecutive years and it was also during this period that just about everyone who could legally purchase a handgun in the United States was legally able to carry one around. Given Lott's conviction that violent crime levels are sensitive to the actual or potential existence of guns in the hands of civilians, the fact that serious crime has stopped declining during the period since 2008 means that Lott's theory as to the causality of crime levels simply cannot be sustained.

So I'll ask this question now for the third time: why let facts get in the way of opinions or a good marketing campaign? If the NRA's goal is to protect the 2nd Amendment by getting more and more people to own guns, then Lott becomes an important resource in the furtherance of that agenda, whether what he says squares with the data or not. But let's stay with this issue a little longer and pose the question from the opposite point of view. What if, rather than guns making us safer, guns actually make us more vulnerable? What if bringing a gun into your home or into some public place doesn't increase the chances of protecting yourself from harm, but instead increases the chances of suffering harm?

This question was asked in the early 90's by Arthur Kellerman and a group of research associates whose work, when it was first published, resulted in two things.[3] First, it was part of the argument that gun control advocates advanced during the debates that led up to passage of the Brady Bill in 1993 and the assault weapons ban the following year. Second, it was scored by the NRA and the pro-gun community as *prime facie* evidence that physicians and public health researchers were using their work to advance an anti-gun agenda which did not deserve government funding since it was not objective research. And while the NRA was successful in restricting CDC funding of any research having to do with guns, Kellerman's early work had already been published, has remained a significant part of the research literature, and continues to shape the gun control side of the debate to this very day. In fact, Lott's book may be seen as almost a conscious effort to rewrite the Kellerman thesis, so let's take some time to figure out what Kellerman was trying to say.

The research that formed the basis of Kellerman's work was a series of interviews conducted with either relatives, close friends or neighbors of 420 people shot to death in their homes located in Seattle, Memphis and Cleveland. These homicides all took place between 1987 and 1992 and interviews with people who knew the victim ("case subjects") and people who lived nearby ("case proxies") were conducted within 30 days after the homicide occurred. The reason why interviews were conducted both with relatives/friends of the deceased as well as with neighbors was to use the responses of the latter as a control on the validity of the testimonies of the former. This approach, known as matched-pairs method, is a standard tool for verifying the content of in-person or interview data.

In sum, Kellerman and his associates found that there were three risk factors that increased the possibility of homicides within the home: illegal drug use, a history of domestic violence and the existence of firearms. The combination of all three factors produced what we might now call a toxic mix, but the existence of any of them created a significant possibility of violent death. The study found exceptions to the overall pattern, in particular cases where either the victim tried, but failed to protect him or herself with a gun, as well as certain "allowable" gun homicides due to the activity of the police.

What is most striking about the data produced by Kellerman and his research team is that even though it was based entirely on homicides that occurred twenty years ago in only three locations over a five-year (or lesser) period, the basic profile of these homicides in terms of identity of victim, reasons for the incident and relationship of attacker to victim are remarkably similar to what is contained in current FBI homicide data for the United States as a whole. For example, two-thirds of the Kellerman victims were male, which is the national average for the gender of homicide victims. Half the homicides resulted from an argument or quarrel, largely the result of domestic conflicts. Again, this is very similar to the current profile. Next, 76% of the victims in this study were killed by someone known to them, which is slightly less than the percentage of current homicides where the two parties had previous knowledge of one another prior to the incident itself. Finally, guns were the weapons used in roughly 50% of the homicides captured in this study, which is somewhat less than the 60% gun-use in current homicides, a not surprising change given how many more guns are floating around than when Kellerman conducted his research twenty years ago.

Kellerman's study was bad news for the NRA because it appeared precisely at the time that the organization's traditional membership—hunters—was aging out and would only be replaced by gun owners whose motives for acquiring guns were conditioned on the belief that personal security and protection from crime necessitated either carrying a gun or keeping one close at hand in the home. Lott might have engendered a much more benign response from his academic adversaries had he stuck to the basic thesis and data of his own approach, without attempting to diminish the findings of Kellerman and others by creating a thoroughly ideological portrait of gun violence that satisfied the NRA's marketing scheme but was and remains devoid of any attention to the facts.

Bear in mind that the fundamental axiom of gun ownership as promoted by the NRA is to always distinguish between "good" guys and "bad" guys. "Good" guys are people who buy and own guns for lawful purposes. And chief among those lawful purposes is protecting themselves and their families from the "bad" guys. That was the rationale for expanding CCW throughout the United States in the 1990's and is what stands behind the demand for "stand your ground" laws today. And not only is self-defense a "good" thing, but as Philip Cook says, using a gun to defend one's family or community the way George Zimmerman defended himself and his community against Trayvon Martin is a "be-knighted" thing; a form of behavior that is both legal, responsible and even patriotic.[4]

Which means that if you pull out your gun in a conscious and justifiable act of self-defense, then by definition the person at whom you point your weapon is a criminal. And here is the point at which

Lott's work breaks down and he reveals himself as someone whose primary goal is to advance the political and marketing agenda of the NRA. Note the following statement: "Criminals are not typical citizens. We know that criminals tend to have low IQs as well as atypical personalities." What Lott is arguing for is the notion that for most of the homicides in which attacker and victim knew each other, which is the majority of all homicides, the actual relationship was between two criminals who got into an argument about something having to do with a criminal act—drugs, theft, etc. They "knew" each other because they had previously been involved in other crimes. This is not, according to Lott, an act that has anything to do with self-defense, nor does it have anything to do with whether guns make us more or less safe. In other words, if you aren't a criminal and you pull out a gun to defend yourself, this makes you a "good" guy. If you're a criminal, then you're a "bad" guy and it doesn't really matter whether you are carrying a gun or not.

Lott and the NRA folks bolster the totally arbitrary distinction between good

guys and bad guys by promoting the work of the other leading NRA scholar, Gary Kleck, who published a study on so-called defensive gun use around the same time Kellerman's study of gun risk first appeared.[5] I'm not going to spend much time on Kleck because I cover his work and the ensuing DGU controversy in *Guns for Good Guys, Guns for Bad Guys*, so here's another plug to go out and buy that book, too. In the meantime, Kleck's work is another effort to justify more gun ownership, but in his case the notion that guns will protect us against crime is explained not by comparing crime trends to the spread of CCW permits, but by examining data that allegedly shows the extent to which Americans were able to make themselves less vulnerable by using a gun before the crime actually occurred, or to put it more precisely, by using a gun to keep a crime from taking place without actually shooting the gun.

It's called defensive gun use, or DGU, and it has become probably the most favored argument of the NRA and their allies for promoting the ownership of more guns. You see, the problem with actually pulling a gun out of your pocket and shooting a bad guy is that from the moment you pull the trigger, lots of people are going to get into the act—the cops, the EMT, maybe the coroner, everyone who was standing around on the corner. It's going to be a big mess. And the worst part is maybe you shouldn't have pulled the trigger at all because maybe the "threat" wasn't such a threat or maybe you just didn't know what you were doing. In 2010 the FBI logged 285 justifiable homicides committed by civilians, a number that has been pretty steady from year to year and, of those homicides, roughly 75% were committed with a gun, again a fairly consistent number from one year to the next.

On the other hand, beginning in the early 1990's, various organizations and gun scholars began publishing estimates about DGUs and, as could be expected, the pro-gun folks presented DGU numbers that were twice to ten times higher than the numbers produced by proponents of more gun control. As I said earlier, I'm not going to discuss the DGU issue in detail because I would just be repeating what you can read in my previous book. But there's another reason that I would prefer not to discuss DGUs any further and that's because in the six months that have passed since I wrote about the DGU issue in *Guns for Good Guys*, I've come to the conclusion that the entire argument is a senseless exercise in hot air. The only reason that scholars like David Hemenway took Gary Kleck and John Lott seriously about DGUs is because academics, particularly those whose research finds its way into serious policy debates, are prone to always assume that an article published in a serious academic journal or a book published by a serious academic press deserve to be reviewed and analyzed in serious terms. Luckily for me, I last held an academic professorship in 1988, so I can afford to decide whether I want to follow academic conventions or not. And in the case of the stupid DGU argument promoted by the NRA and their research acolytes like Kleck and Lott, I prefer to dismiss such intellectual junk out of hand, call it what it is—the work of charlatans—and get on to more serious stuff.

And the reason I call proponents of DGUs charlatans is because they are trying to make a logical argument out of whole cloth. The truth is that there has never been a single DGU proponent who has ever figured out, never mind even attempted to come up with a method that would independently verify or validate the alleged DGU incidents which they claim take place several million times each year. Remember, we are not talking about a single instance in which a gun actually went off. Roughly 15 percent of the respondents to Kleck's survey said that a gun (their gun) went off, but not a single participant in these surveys could produce a single bit of real evidence to back up their claims. *Nor were they asked to produce any evidence!* What they were asked was whether or not the fact that they had a gun resulted in what otherwise would have been a criminal act not taking place. And if Kleck and Lott are correct in stating that DGUs take place more than several million times each year, then all of a sudden it turns out that the only reason that our crime rate isn't sky high compared to other advanced countries is because all these good guys and a few good girls are walking around town with their guns.

Lott uses the DGU argument to discredit Kellerman's findings by saying that even if the existence of guns increases the risk of homicide, it also increases the possibility of a successful DGU, thereby negating the risk and, given the high number of DGUs found by Kleck and others, actually tilts the value of gun ownership back towards a safer and less vulnerable environment the more that people opt to own guns. But the real problem with Lott's method is that even if there was a general confluence between more guns on the one hand and less crime on the other, we still don't know whether or not there's any connection between those two trends, for the simple reason that the people whose views on this issue need to be gathered, analyzed and understood are the ones whose decisions to use or not use a gun created the whole debate in the first place.

The fact is that Lott never interviewed a single person who, according to him, made a decision to *not* use a gun because of the possibility that the intended victim might have been armed. For that matter, neither Kellerman nor any member of his research team ever spoke to either a victim, because they were all dead, or an individual whose behavior reflected the increased risk of violence because of the existence of a gun. So here we have a rather tendentious and polemical debate about guns and gun violence that has been going on for more than twenty years, and yet the people whose actions and behavior create the reason for the debate in the first place never seem to appear. Why did gun victimization drop so drastically between 1993 and 2001? Since we know that it wasn't because there were less guns available for use during those years, we have to assume that a certain number of individuals made the decision to do whatever it was they wanted to do without using a gun. And let's go a little further and assume that in many cases the point was never reached where using a gun came into the picture, because what led up to that decision—an argument, a crime, a whatever it was—simply didn't take place.

A study that followed Kellerman's methodology was conducted in Philadelphia by a faculty team led by Charles Branas from the University of Pennsylvania Medical School, which attempted to analyze the links, if any, between gun possession and gun assaults covering 677 individuals who had been shot but not killed between 2003 and 2006.[6] Like the Kellerman study, interviews were conducted both with case and control participants, the latter group being interviewed within two days of the shooting, whereas information about the case participants (the actual victims) was derived from police and investigator reports. In order to make the information about each case as comprehensive and reliable as possible, the researchers created a conceptual framework to serve as a guide for the collection and analysis of data generated by the research:

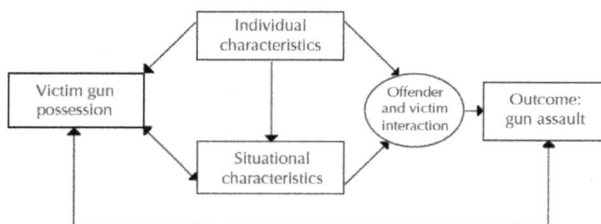

Note that each case began with verifying whether the victim did or did not possess a gun. To this information was then added individual characteristics of the participants (age, gender, etc.) and situational characteristics of the assault (where, when, how, etc.), which was then tied to the interaction between the shooter and victim (provoked or unprovoked, degree of resistance, etc.) leading up to the assault itself. The findings in this study correlated even more strongly than Kellerman's work as regards the link between someone possessing a gun and ending up being the victim of an assault. And not surprisingly, Lott and others who favor more guns have criticized this research as also undercounting the degree to which ownership of a gun can protect, rather than provoke an attack. But once again, although Branas and his colleagues have marshaled their facts and presented their findings in a diligent and persuasive way, the gap between what the evidence may suggest as opposed to what we still don't really understand is very wide. And the reason for the gap is not difficult to figure out when you consider that the researchers created both case and control groups by looking at the people who got shot. The fact is that if 677 residents of Philadelphia between 2003 and 2006 decided to pull out a gun and begin at some point to bang away, there had to be at least that many people in similar circumstances who kept their guns hidden instead.

Notwithstanding my harsh words for Lott, Kleck and all the other NRA sycophants who want to help promote gun sales by injecting their own gun fantasies into an arena in which serious and honest debate should occur, I'll be the first to admit that there are certainly times when having access to a gun might be a very good thing. I'm thinking, for example, of the incident that occurred in New York City on September 29, 2013, when a gang of bikers chased a family SUV, forced the vehicle off the highway, then surrounded the car and threatened to beat up the driver unless he handed them his cash. Incidentally, the incident took place in broad daylight, and much of it was recorded on a phone and then uploaded to YouTube for everyone to see.

Perhaps the driver of the SUV was a little too aggressive when he found himself first entangled with the bikers on the West Side Highway, and perhaps the cops might have been more diligent or responded more quickly when the 911 call was first sent out. But the bottom line is that the driver of the car was menaced by a gang and eventually hauled from the vehicle and beaten pretty badly on a Manhattan street in the middle of the afternoon. Would the gang have backed off if he had pulled a gun? Are there times you feel that having a gun in your pocket would have made you feel less vulnerable or scared? I have never feared for my life or my person walking down any street in the United States, but I also don't believe that people who actually use a gun in self defense are necessarily doing the wrong thing. Sometimes crazy things can happen, like the guy in Florida who fired through his door at what he thought was an intruder when it turned out that the guy trying to break into his house was an alligator. And sometimes tragic things happen, like the incident in Georgia where a homeowner mistakenly killed a 72-year-old Alzheimer's patient who wouldn't respond to the man's demands to clear out of his back yard. But most people, average people, tend to be reasonable and can usually be trusted to do the reasonable thing, not only with guns but with everything else. The problem, however, is that putting a gun together with someone who isn't reasonable just can't end up being a good thing. And here's an example of why:

On January 13, 2014, Chad and Nicole Oulson dropped off their three-year-old daughter at a daycare and drove from their home near Tampa, Florida to see the movie *Lone Survivor*, at a mall theater in the nearby town of Wesley Chapel. During the coming attractions, Oulson took out his cell and began exchanging text messages to the daughter's babysitter but was interrupted by a another patron occupying a seat behind Oulson who objected to the texting activity, even though the main feature was not yet showing on the screen. I wasn't in the theater, but I don't recall ever going to a movie and worrying about making noise during the previews which is usually when people are moving around, commenting back and forth, sharing snacks and, by and large, not overly concerned about making noise.

It is not clear how Oulson first responded to the request to shut down his text activity, but we do know that the person who made the demand was a 71-year-old retired police captain from the Tampa P.D. who was also at the movie with his wife. The cop's name was Curtis Reeves. He had earlier in his career been responsible for developing and training the Tampa SWAT team, and his son, Matthew, was a Tampa cop. In any case, after demanding that Oulson discontinue his texting activity, Reeves got up, went out to the lobby and allegedly complained to theater management, who evidently refused to intervene. At which point Reeves returned to his seat, demanded again that Oulson cease texting, a few nasty words went back and forth, Oulson stood up and threw something at Reeves who, fearing that he was about to be seriously attacked, pulled out a pistol and shot Oulson to death. When police arrived, one of whom by coincidence was the shooter's son Matthew, his father was sitting calmly in his seat and surrendered after a brief tussle with another deputy over whether or not he had to give up his gun. In the aftermath of the shooting, the ex-cop's attorney claims he will portray his client as being innocent because he "stood his ground" in the face of a deadly attack, what the local media is now calling The Popcorn Defense.

This incident contains all the elements that allow us to understand and evaluate the issue of guns protecting us from other guns (or, in this case, from a bag of popcorn) that has been the main driver of pro-gun advocacy over the last several decades. First, the incident happened in a large, public location where other shootings, including some of the worst mass shootings have taken place (read: Aurora, Colorado in July, 2012). Second, the shooter was a highly experienced firearms instructor who had been carrying a gun for virtually all of his adult life. Finally, despite some post-incident comments that indicated he had previously objected to someone texting in the same theater at a previous point in time, there was nothing in his background or his previous behavior which indicated that he was a risk because he was walking around with a gun. In other words, if you are going to go along with the NRA dictum that "the only thing that can stop a bad guy with a gun is a good guy with a gun," then the retired cop Curtis Reeves represented the archetypical good guy. Except the other guy didn't have a gun. He had a bag of popcorn. And that's exactly why the notion that guns can protect us against other guns is just so much BS.

Here's the question to ask about what happened at the movie theater Wesley Chapel, a question which, as far as I can tell, wasn't asked by anyone either involved with, or commenting on the episode: what would the ex-cop turned shooter named Curtis Reeves have done if he hadn't been carrying a gun? Actually, it's what he first did: he walked out to the lobby and asked the theater manager to intervene. And when the manager refused, Reeves at this point could have either gone back to seat and kept his mouth shut while Oulson continued to text until the feature attraction started up, or could have gone back to his seat, grabbed his wife and moved to another seat. I should add, by the way, that when asked to stop texting, Oulson could have been a gentleman and complied with Reeves's demand. But Oulson was younger, bigger, and tougher, and nobody was going to tell *him* that he couldn't continue to do whatever he goddamn well pleased to do until the main feature began.

So here we have the typical, all-American, *fuck me? fuck you!* scenario that takes place somewhere every day, or maybe every minute of every day because that would add up to 1,440 arguments each day and in a country of 312 million people that's not such a big deal. But it is a big deal if you're the guy or the girl with the bag of popcorn and the other guy or girl has a gun. Because in 2012 more than 5,000 residents of the United States were shot to death simply because a few fuck you's got out of hand. That's right, according to the FBI, the motive in more than 50% of all homicides committed with firearms wasn't robbery, wasn't a drug deal gone bad, wasn't even a drive-by shooting. It was one too many fuck you's.

The reason I have gone into such lengths to explain what happened in the movie theater near Tampa is that when we talk about violence, particularly violence that goes to the extreme of involving a gun, we never think about retired cops like Curtis Reeves because they aren't "bad" guys and it's the "bad" guys who are the only ones responsible for unauthorized uses of a gun. A study by the Department of Justice found in 2002 that 66% of the individuals convicted for murder had a previous arrest record, which means that one-third of the people who committed murder were new to the game and only became "bad guys" after the murder, followed by their arrest and conviction. Given the seriousness of homicide, you would think that virtually everyone who killed someone else had previously been involved in some kind of serious crime. But at least one-third of all murderers were like Lenny and his buddy, whose murder of Lenny's great-uncle for fifty bucks was the story with which this book first began.

People like Lenny and the other 3,500+ individuals without previous criminal records who murdered other people may have started walking around with a gun because they had some idea that it would protect them against crime. In fact, all the gun did was give them the opportunity to use it for reasons which we still haven't been able to explain. And neither has anyone who promotes the idea that guns protect us from crime been able to explain why guns are often used to commit the worst and most violent crime of all.

The NRA would like you to believe that when it comes to the *when* of gun violence, that this can be explained by dividing everyone who uses a gun into two, very distinct and easily understood groups. On the one hand we have the "bad guys" who use guns to commit crimes. Now in fact it turns out that a majority of gun homicides grow out of long standing, continuous disputes between individuals who not only know each other but have previously fought and argued without the benefit of a gun. So if you are going to paint everyone who uses a gun to commit a crime as someone who made a conscious decision to carry a weapon because it was a tool of his trade, it's an argument that may go over with all those law-abiding gun owners out there but it's simply not true.

As for the idea that there are all these "good guys" walking around with guns whose armed status is protecting us against crime, the evidence supporting this assertion is even less capable of passing any validation test than the data that shows that gun crimes are only committed by criminals who, in the process of committing a crime, consciously choose to use a gun. The argument that concealed carry permits are a causal factor in crime decline is based on coincidence which is half-baked at best; the estimates of millions of defensive gun uses don't meet even the most minimal requirements for assuming that what someone said in a voice survey bears any relationship to truth or facts.

Just as I was finishing the pre-publication editing of this book, a study on the effect of concealed-carry and gun violence has appeared, and deserves some mention here.[7] The study covered a 48-month period, divided between 24 months before and after a new law on regulating concealed carry was enacted in Arizona. Actually, the new law more or less de-regulated concealed carry, removing both the requirement that a gun-owner possess a separate concealed-carry permit as well as removing the requirement that someone who wants to walk around with a concealed weapon needed to certify that he/she had taken a proficiency course in using the weapon. Basically, the new law now allows anyone who can legally own a gun in Arizona to walk around with it on their person.

And what did the new study conducted by a group of ER and Trauma doctors show? It showed that in Tucson, where the study was conducted, intentional gun-related injuries and deaths as a proportion of all violent crime remained about the same, but the proportion of gun-related homicides went up. Statewide, if we look at crime numbers from the FBI, the murder rate went down between 2010 and 2012, but the rape, robbery and aggravated assault rate went up, and the overall rate of violent crime, notwithstanding the drop in the homicide rate, also went up. Under the new law, Arizonans can walk around with a concealed weapon not only without any training in how to use the gun, but also without having to undergo a background check in order to acquire the gun. By eliminating a separate concealed carry permit requirement, Arizona basically agreed with people like Lott, Kleck and the rest of the NRA gang that carrying a gun for self-defense is something that everyone should do without having to be qualified at all. There's only one little problem: the law lets a lot more people join the ranks of the NRA's good guys, but the bad guys seem to be winning the fight.

But let's play devil's advocate and assume for a moment that there is some truth to the bad-guy, good-guy gun mantra promoted by the NRA. Where do we fit the nearly 20,000 suicides that take place each year whose perpetrators end their lives with guns? And the number of successful suicides is dwarfed by the much larger number of individuals who, like the retired cop I'm going to tell you about in Chapter 5, came literally within an inch of committing the ultimate act of gun violence using his own gun to take his own life. On a blog I wrote recently about this issue a stalwart NRA member posted the following: "Mike—how can you advocate controlling someone's access to guns when nobody has the right to tell someone else whether or not they can take their own life?" If that's what the argument about gun violence is reduced to, let's stop the argument right here.

Notes to Chapter 2

1. John R. Lott, Jr., More Guns, Less Crime, 3rd edn., (Chicago, 2010.)

2. Franklin Zimring, The City That Became Safe (New York, 2012.)

3. Arthur L. Kellerman, "Gun Ownership As a Risk Factor For Homicide In The Home," New England Journal of Medicine, 329, 15 (October 7, 1993) 1084-1091; and Sripal Bangalore, et. al., "Gun Ownership and Firearm-related Deaths," The American Journal of Medicine, 126, 10 (April, 2013), 873-876.

4. Philip J. Cook, "The Great American Gun War: Notes From Four Decades in the Trenches," Chicago, 2013 (forthcoming in Volume 42, Crime and Justice in America).

5. Gary Kleck and Marc Gertz, "Armed Resistance to Crime: The Prevalence and Nature of Self-Defense With a Gun," Journal of Criminal Law and Criminology, 86, 1 (1995).

6. Charles C. Branas, et. al., "Investigating the Link Between Gun Possession and Gun Assault," American Journal of Public Health, 99, 11 (November, 2009), 2034-2040.

7. R. Ginwalla, et. al., "Repeal of the Concealed Weapons Law and its Impact on gun-related injuries and deaths," Trauma and Acute Care Surgery, 76, 3 (March, 2014) 569-575.

CHAPTER 3

HERE'S WHAT HAPPENS WHEN YOU PULL THE TRIGGER

I was always a nine freak. Gun people will immediately understand what I mean by that expression, but for the non-gunnies who are reading this book I'd better explain. My first real gun, which I bought when I was twelve years old, was a revolver that shot either 38 Special or plain old 38. I don't remember which because my great-uncle Nathan took the gun away from me and pawned it in a shop on Davie Boulevard near Pompano Beach before I ever got a chance to shoot it. Not that I even thought about shooting the gun for the thirty minutes or so that it was in my possession. If you've read *Guns for Good Guys* you know I bought the gun for fifty bucks at a flea market in Florida somewhere in the glades off of Highway 441. What you don't know until now is that Nathan not only pawned it an hour later but also kept the cash. What was he going to do? Put me on a train back to New York where, when I arrived and was met by my parents at Pennsylvania Station I would walk up to them and present them with a gun? Hi Mom, Hi Dad, look what I brought back from Florida. It was 1956 and I was twelve years old. Yea, that would have gone over big.

I bought my next gun in Covington, Kentucky, when I was twenty years old. I had dropped out of college in Cincinnati and was working across the river in a shingle factory in Covington, pulling shingles for the P.J. Carey Co., which ran three shifts to meet the demand for home-building products and couldn't care who you were or what jail had just released you as long as you would show up and stack shingles three-square deep as they came off the mill. I got really lucky after a few days and when the foreman, Slim, a dumb redneck if there ever was one with a toothpick in one corner of his mouth and a cigarette in the other, asked if anyone wanted to get off the line and go work with "that boy Gladys over there," I couldn't wait to tear off my mill gloves and get away from the line. "That boy Gladys" was, in fact, a black man of indeterminate age who drove a truck around the plant picking up garbage and hauling it out to the dump.

For whatever reason, maybe because I was the only white worker who didn't mind sitting in a truck next to a black, my new friend Gladys, whose last name was Turner, took a liking to me and later that week invited me home after the shift to eat dinner and meet "Maw." Who it turned out was a white woman also of indeterminate age, and I suspect that I might have been the first white man to spend an evening in the Turner residence because, if I'm not mistaken, interracial marriages were probably still against the law in Kentucky in the year of our Lord 1963.

At some point during or after dinner the talk got around to guns and Gladys showed me a big Colt revolver that he always kept out at night next to his bed. Can't be too careful, he said to me, as we passed the beautiful piece back and forth. And what's the first thing you say when someone opens a drawer and pulls out a gun? If you don't know the answer you probably don't know all that much about guns, so I'll tell it to you now: you ask if the guy has any more. Which he did. In fact old Gladys had four or five more and then one thing led to another and I had a paycheck coming in a day or two, and when I left the Turner residence that evening I was carrying a beautiful Browning nine. Plus a box or two of ammunition. Like Gladys said, can't be too careful and what's the point of having a gun if it's going to sit around all empty inside?

My Hi-Power or one of my Hi-Powers

Ever since I got that first nine from Gladys I've gone out of my way to buy and own just about every nine-millimeter pistol I could find. I've cut back a little lately, but I still have a bunch of nines including a Browning Hi-Power pistol that looks exactly like the one I bought from Gladys in 1963. The Browning I now own was made at the Fabrique National factory in Belgium in 1968, which is where this remarkable little mechanical device was manufactured from when it was first produced in 1935 until the company moved the manufacturing plant to Portugal in order to save some dough and in the process, by the way, ruined the quality and the workmanship of the gun.

And why do I say that the gun was a remarkable mechanical device? Because how else can you describe a piece of metal whose movable parts can withstand the equivalent of 11,000 pounds of pressure every time a round goes off and a bullet runs up the snout? Try dropping your iPad on the floor a few times and see what happens. And not only did I shoot the Hi-Power I got from Gladys more than a few thousand times without ever having a jam, but I also did all that shooting almost for free because the way the Hi-Power was designed by that remarkable genius named John Browning, if you take a 115-grain, round-nose bullet and stick it onto a 9mm brass case, it doesn't even matter how much powder you use, as long as the bullet can be crimped (which means tightened) in the case before you load the round into the mag. Which means that if you don't have any money, you don't need to buy factory-made ammunition. All you need to do is get a little hand reloading kit, a one-time purchase of about twenty bucks, and bring the kit, a can of powder, bullets and some new primers along to the range, and after you shoot a mag full of factory rounds, and a Browning mag holds 14 rounds, you can just sit there, scoop up the brass, run each piece of fired brass through your little reloading kit and you've got another mag-full of ammo to shoot for about one-tenth the cost of Winchester or Remington or Federal rounds.

And here's the real beauty of the whole scheme: if you use a 115-grain bullet, you don't have to measure how much powder you put in the case. And it doesn't even matter whether you use handgun powder, rifle powder, the slow-burning stuff, the fast-ignition stuff or whatever. If the reloaded cartridge will fit in the mag, it will fit in the gun. And it will work every time. Like the ad for those Timex watches used to say: takes a licking and keeps on ticking. So I used to go to the range, or to a sandpit near my house when I lived down South, and I would just sit there all afternoon, shooting, scooping and shooting again. And believe me when I tell you that I wasn't the one who discovered how easy it was to make ammunition for this gun. It was designed that way because Browning knew that what made a gun really valuable was not whether the wood had a beautiful finish, not whether the metal had a lovely sheen. What made a gun valuable was if it worked—worked every time you took it out, no matter what. And so he designed two pistols that always worked: the Colt 45 pistol aka 1911, and then the Hi-Power nine. And why did he use these two calibers? Because he knew that the way he engineered his guns, no matter how much pressure was created by the round going off, the slide would slip back, eject the spent shell and ram a new shell into the breech every single time.

The Colt .45. Still going strong after 113 years.

I also owned a lot of 1911 pistols over the years, have two or three lying around now, but I never had the kind of love affair with the *quarenta y cinco* that I still have with my nines. Which is just my own personal affectation, nothing more than that. Last year I finally broke down and bought my first Glock. Why did I wait so long to buy the only handgun whose design is the first truly new engineering concept in more than sixty years? Because I didn't want to be like everyone else who's just got to have a Glock. So I waited and eventually got myself the little compact 9mm called the Model 26. But the company makes 4 different pistols in 9 millimeter and how long did it take me to also get my hands on a Model 17, a Model 19 and a Model 34? Not very long.

The point of all this is to make you understand that when we talk about gun violence (how do I say the following without sounding like a high-minded jerk?), we're not talking about some academic theory or intellectual exercise that may or may not be valid or true. We're talking about a gun: how it works and what happens when it works. Because you can stand all day at a shooting range, shooting at targets and it doesn't mean very much at all. You aim the gun, pull the trigger, feel the recoil and a little hole appears on a piece of paper somewhere in front of your face. Or maybe you go out to a sand pit or into the woods, stick up a couple of empty bottles (full bottles are more fun, actually), pull the trigger and almost immediately the glass splatters and the bottle disappears. You can now even buy 3D torso targets made out of plastic and foam which produce a little bit of red paint at the entrance-point and kind of creates the feeling of a video game except you're using a real gun.

And here's where we're going with all this and, believe me, I sat very still in front of my word processor thinking about the next sentence and what it would really mean. So here goes: You don't really know what a gun is all about until you see what it does when the bullet that comes out of its barrel and collides with human flesh. Because here's the dirty little secret about guns and the bullets they shoot: they do what I just said—collide with human flesh—better than anything else. A little further on in this chapter we're going to compare what happens to human flesh when it's hit with a bullet as opposed to being punctured with a knife or whacked with a club. If you're not an ER physician you might have a bit of trouble looking at some of the picture and reading some of the text that will shortly appear. But if you haven't figured it out by now let me break it to you gently: the whole point of this book is not to add yet another volume to the already-overloaded shelf of advocacy books about guns. I don't have a "solution" to the "problem" and I don't really care. You want to come to my gun shop, buy a gun, take it out and blow your head off or someone else's head off, it's really no business of mine and I make no value judgments either way. But the truth is that I have never read a book about guns that explains what they're about by putting you, the reader, right behind the guy who's going to pull that trigger. What does he see, what does he think, and what actually happens in the moment just before and just after he uses the gun? That's what the rest of this book is all about, and we're going to start by taking it in reverse order and first considering what happens after the gun goes off.

Which brings us back to the 9 millimeter round. Because it's the cartridge, the shape, weight and speed that really determines what happens when it collides with human flesh. And of all the rounds that are out there I like the 9 most of all because of what we refer to as its yaw. But before we talk about yaw, we have to introduce a bit (but not too much) of physics into the discussion, beginning with the notion of kinetic energy. Remember that when a bullet hits any object it is travelling at a certain speed. In most cases, the speed is determined by the weight and size of the bullet, the power of the explosion that pushed the bullet out of the barrel, and the length of the barrel through which the bullet travelled. The greater the force of the explosion, the faster the bullet will travel as it leaves the barrel and the longer the barrel the greater the acceleration of the bullet, because the gas created by the explosion of the gun powder has more time to burn and create more pressure which pushes the bullet out faster. So, for example, a 38-caliber bullet weighing 124 grains will leave a 4-inch barrel at roughly 1,000 feet per second, but will exit from a 6-inch barrel at 1,300 feet per second.[1]

Once the bullet leaves the barrel it will begin slowing down due to the force of friction, especially since the bullet is spinning (so that it will travel accurately). Now here's where we have to introduce a bit of physics. Kinetic energy is the amount of energy required to accelerate a body (the bullet) to its stated velocity which can be represented as one-half mass times velocity squared. The moment that the bullet reaches its stated velocity, friction and gravity take over and unless additional energy is transferred to the bullet it will slow down and eventually drop to the ground. Now remember that the whole point of shooting a gun is to get the bullet to hit an object and, since we are assuming that the intended object is another person, we want the collision between bullet and object to create as much damage as possible.

The damage we are talking about involves blood, tissue and bones which, taken together, are the basic physiological components of the human body and which, when damaged to a certain degree, will result in the inability of the body to function in a normal way. Thus, if a solid object cuts through tissue there will be immediate blood loss, depending on where the solid object hits, which will then reduce the functioning of the organs that depend on the flow of blood, which leads to a lack of functions controlled by those particular organs. If the solid object hits tissue which happens to be one of the vital organs itself, such as the brain or the heart, the loss of blood and the functional failure of the particular organ becomes much more serious.

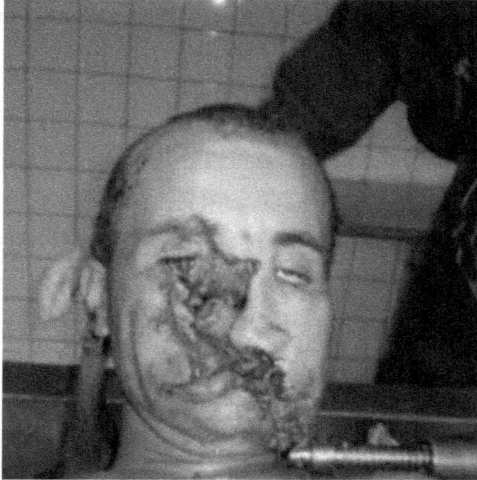

This guy's dead. Not because of the loss of blood in and of itself, but because the solid object ripped through layers of tissue, much of it connected to internal organs that immediately shut down, leading to a massive failure of the normal physiological functions that keep us all alive. What you can't see in this picture was the result of what I mentioned earlier, the kinetic force of the bullet, because as the bullet enters the body most of its kinetic force creates a wound cavity that is briefly much larger than the size of the bullet itself. And it is the size of this cavity that creates blood loss, organ malfunction and either serious injury or death.

There are also secondary factors to be considered about gun wounds which make them even more severe than what happens in and around the point where the bullet first hits flesh. Because bullets travel at a very high speed, the fact that the initial penetration creates a massive, interior wound cavity doesn't mean that all the kinetic energy has been used up. The bullet may initially penetrate the chest, for example, then hit a rib and tear through the abdomen and lodge in a leg. So now we have three different wounds that are creating tissue damage and blood loss, and taking care of one wound doesn't in any way make things more stable in other parts of the body that the bullet tore through. Which means the medical response to this event, if there is a medical response, must be more skilled and much more intense than the response to a simple physical wound, such as getting hit with what the cops like to call a 'blunt object' like a baseball bat, a tire iron or a club.

But before we begin to compare different kinds of wounds, take a look at the picture below:

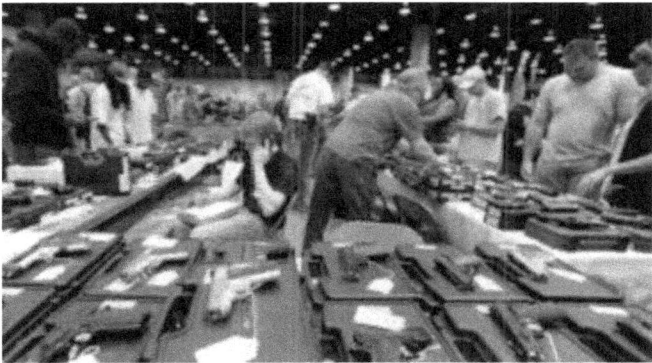

I grabbed this pic from a National Public Radio website that was doing a series of reports on guns. It's similar to pictures we have all seen in media outlets like The New York Times, The Washington Post and other journalistic venues which have run countless articles about gun violence since the massacre at Sandy Hook. If all those reporters and pundits knew anything at all about gun violence or, for that matter, about guns, they would demand that their publishers run a picture like the one of the dead guy that appears back on Page 102. Because until you look at a picture of someone who really was shot with a gun, you're off into a discussion that may have very little to do with the reality of gun violence. And this brings me all the way back to what I said at the beginning of this chapter when I talked about the 9 millimeter round in terms of its yaw.

The yaw of a bullet is the degree to which it sways to and fro as it moves forward from the exit point of a barrel to the entrance point of the body. Bullets are designated by their diameter at the widest point, which in the case of a nine means $9/100^{ths}$ of a meter. Bullet diameters can be expressed either metrically or by decimals, usually depending on whether the cartridge was first developed over here or over there. The 9 millimeter was developed over there in Europe, so it carries the metric designation. The

45, on the other hand, was developed over here, and its diameter is $45/100^{ths}$ of an inch. What's interesting about the nine is that of all the standard handgun calibers it tends to have the greatest degree of yaw. So when it hits the body, the wound cavity isn't just the size of the bullet's diameter enlarged by the amount of kinetic energy transferred at the moment of impact; the cavity is even larger because the bullet is entering the body at an angle which makes its effective diameter much greater than 9 millimeters. So what happens is that if you use a nine, like my Glock 26 for example, you get a lot more blood for the buck.

You probably get just as much or more kinetic energy if you move up to the 40-caliber ammunition, like the 40 S&W or the venerable 45. But the reason I really love the nine is because once you get into the 40s, the size and the weight of the bullet creates a lot more reverse pressure at the moment of ignition (when the round goes off), and the recoil, depending on the design of the gun, can be pretty fierce. That's the reason why the truly greatest and most versatile handgun cartridge of all time, the 357 Magnum, never caught on with police. Because in addition to the possibility that the bullet's extreme speed would result in severe damage to an innocent bystander who was hundreds of yards away from the muzzle of the gun, even in the most experienced hands the recoil makes it extremely difficult to get off a well-placed, quick second shot.

Firearm cartridges are like software, no one type of bullet or caliber can do everything equally well. So if you're going to walk around with a banger and it's going to be used for the real reason that these things were invented, ultimately you have to come up with some degree of compromise which lets you use the gun effectively in as many different situations as possible. And remember, when we use a word like "effective," we're not talking about knocking a few beer cans off of a wall. We're talking about knocking off someone's head, or their arm, or some other part of their body because that's what your gun was really designed to do.

Which is why the 9mm caliber has probably been the most popular pistol round of all time, even more popular than the 45, precisely because it isn't the biggest and it isn't the best, but it does enough things well to be adaptable to so many guns. Which doesn't necessarily mean that it's the caliber of choice when we get down to the street. Because as I'm going to discuss shortly, the bigger the caliber usually means the more expensive the gun, usually but not always. On the other hand, if the person walking around with the gun knows anything about what he's carrying, he's going to know that you can do a lot more damage with a 9mm than with a smaller caliber like a 22. The problem with the little 22 is that it hits with high speed but it's a very small shell. So it will penetrate but the wound cavity won't be very large because a bullet that only weighs 40 grains or so doesn't need a lot of ignition pressure to run out of a barrel at a medium-high (1,000 feet per second) speed. Where a 22-caliber bullet becomes a real killing piece is when it sits on top of a 223 brass case, weighs 55 or 60 grains and leaves an AR-15 or M-16 rifle at 3,000 feet per second or more. But since rifles are to street killings like oil is to water (as in the two have very little to do with one another), we can leave the discussion of rifle ballistics to another time.

Back in 1995 the Bureau of Justice Statistics published an article that detailed the kinds of guns and calibers that were used in crimes. The data covered close to a million guns that were reported stolen which, given the fact that the FBI was receiving 275,000 stolen gun reports each year, seems to indicate that the data covered possibly four separate years. The most popular gun and caliber reported stolen during those years was the revolver in 38 special caliber, not surprising because until the early 90's, this was probably the most popular weapon for civilians and was the gun carried by more than

90% of all uniformed police. One-fifth of all guns stolen were of this type, another 11 percent were revolvers in 22 caliber and another 11 percent were 357 mag wheel guns. On the pistol side the most popular caliber was 9mm (9%) followed closely by 25 caliber (8%) and 22 (7%.)

The mid-90's marked the point at which handgun owners were all making the transition from revolvers to pistols, which was also reflected in the fact that the manufacture of pistols was outpacing revolvers by a margin of two or three to one. The problem was that stolen guns and crime guns aren't necessarily the same thing, and the data in the BJS report on guns used in crimes covered only guns recovered from crimes in Philadelphia, some parts of Virginia and Hawaii, with 9mm pistols appearing more frequently than in the data on stolen guns, but not yet as popular as revolvers chambered for the 38.

We do have some good data from California, however, which seems to indicate that the identity of stolen guns and the identity of crime guns is more or less the same.[2] Here's a graph from 2012 covering 134 weapons that were used in crimes:

Weapons by Caliber

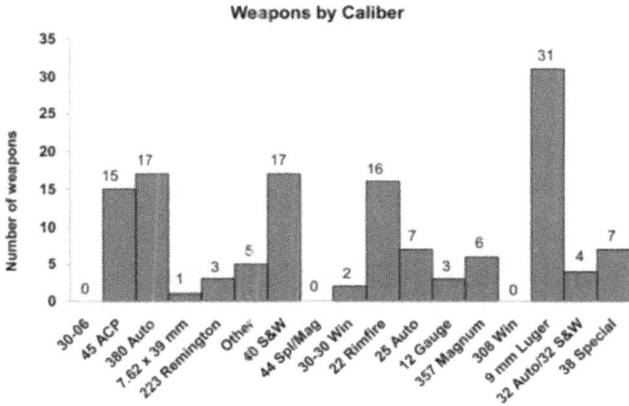

Taken together, more than half the guns analyzed for this report were in heavy pistol calibers—45, 40 and 9. The agency reporting this data, the California Bureau of Forensic Services, tends to work on guns that are recovered in the more rural areas and smaller towns. Which probably means that in a big city like Los Angeles the tendency towards high-caliber pistols would be even more pronounced. But either way, what this report reflects, compared to the data from the 1990's, is the degree to which people who are using guns to commit crimes are just as much aware of changes in the market and technologies of handguns as people who acquire guns through legal means.

So now we know what guns are out there and we know what they can do. So here's where it gets really interesting. Ready? In 1972 an economist named

Franklin Zimring conducted some very detailed research covering more than 1,000 gun assaults in Chicago, which included more than 150 fatalities.[3] While the percentage of fatal attacks (15%) was significantly higher than what we find to be the overall percentage today (3%,) this ratio of fatal to non-fatal gun assaults can be found in many urban areas. Furthermore, the homicide rate was five times higher with guns than with knives, which is almost exactly the same gun-knife ratio reported nationally over the last several years by the FBI. Even though Zimring's data is now more than forty years old, the similarity between what he found for Chicago and what holds true in more recent studies leads me to believe that we can use his findings to posit some possible answers to the question which keeps floating around this book, namely, why do people use guns?

The first key finding by Zimring was the extent to which circumstances surrounding non-fatal and fatal gun attacks were similar; i.e., the latter events more often than not grew out of the former—fights and arguments were the primary cause for both fatal and non-fatal shootings. The second most important finding was the clear difference between non-fatal and fatal gun attacks based on caliber of the weapon, and this held true both for single as well as multiple wound attacks. Overall, victims shot with high-caliber guns were twice as likely to die as victims who received gun shots from smaller calibers, particularly 22, and this ratio held true both for single-shot attacks as well as for attacks that produced multiple wounds.

The most important finding from the study, however, was that Zimring could discern a pattern of intention based on the number of wounds per shooting, a pattern at variance with most of the extant literature on homicidal intentions or motives. In brief, most criminal sociologists had assumed that homicide had its own motivations and explanations, quite distinct and autonomous from the circumstances and intentionality of generalized violence. Zimring's careful research, on the other hand, clearly develops the possibility that homicidal violence is just another form of random, unintentional violence in which the possibility of causing death is recognized, particularly because of the choice of weapon, but the actual resultant death is not the primary reason for the assault. And what drives this conclusion is the fact that in 62 percent of all fatal gun assaults and 72 percent of non-fatal assaults, the attacker ceased the attack after hitting the victim with only one shot, even though in most cases he could have continued to pull the trigger and inflict more harm. This is where the importance of different calibers cannot be discounted because if the purpose of the attack is to simply cause injury without being overly concerned about whether the Injury is fatal or not, then showing up for the fight with a heavy caliber weapon means that the resultant violence will be more serious, with a level of damage that may or may not have anything to do with the intentions of the shooter.

The intentions of the shooter. We still don't know what's going on in the brain of the person holding the gun just before it goes *bang*. Maybe, as Zimring's evidence suggests (and there have been additional studies that suggest much the same thing), there was little or anything of conscious, premeditated thoughts going on about either the intended or the unintended results of the gun going off. If this is true, then we cannot escape some important considerations about the why of gun violence which are as follows.

First, the fact that gun violence is the most destructive and lethal form of violence doesn't necessarily mean that people who shoot other people with guns are necessarily the most violent or the most destructive members of society. We treat them that way in terms of punishments, but even though the punishment may "fit" the crime, it doesn't necessarily explain the crime. This may sound quite stupid and/or naïve, but the fact that someone puts a gun in their pocket and walks down the street doesn't necessarily mean that he's thought out the consequences of actually pulling the weapon out and using it. He may be carrying the gun because he wants to show it to someone else, or because it's "cool" to walk around with a gun, or because who the hell knows for what reason.

The real problem with Zimring's data is that it covers a time when most of the guns that are now used in shootings didn't exist, or if they did exist they hadn't yet gotten into the street. Back in the 1970's, large-caliber handguns were almost exclusively six-shot revolvers, and almost all of the pistols floating around were small-caliber, concealable 22s or 25s. High-capacity, heavy caliber pistols like Glock and Sig were not yet on the market, Browning HiPower and Beretta pistols were rarely imported, and the second most popular handgun cartridge, the 40 S&W, didn't yet exist. So it's difficult to move the Zimring theory of non-causality of gun violence into the present without having some more current data on exactly what happens when someone pulls out a gun.

Actually, I have such data, but it fits better into one of the later chapters below. For the moment let's stick with Zimring and get back to my unending search to talk about gun violence in terms of *why*. Now that we have finished three chapters, it is clear that there is precious little we don't know about gun violence in terms of who uses guns, where they use them and against whom they use them. Thanks to the NRA's attempt to promote near-universal gun ownership there's a big argument about the when, but whether or not you're convinced that we can break the gun world down neatly into bad guys and good guys, there's plenty of data to prove or disprove that issue as well.

Notes to Chapter 3

1. Much of the technical information which follows is drawn from, among other sources, V. Di Maio, M.D., *Gunshot Wounds – Practical Aspects of Firearms, Ballistics, and Forensic Techniques* (Boca Raton, 1999) and Jan Leestma, *Forensic Neuropathology* (Boca Raton, 2009).

2. Office of the Attorney General, California Department of Justice, "Firearms Used in the Commission of Crimes, 2009."

3. F. Zimring, "The Medium is the Message: Firearm Caliber as a Determinant of Death from Assault," *The Journal of Legal Studies*, 1, 1 (Jan., 1972) 97-123.

CHAPTER 4

THE GREAT AMERICAN CRIME GAME

In the previous chapters we covered the *what,* the *when* and the *why* of gun violence. Now it's time to look at the *where.* Let's go back to the map on Page 31 and examine the data on which it is based in some detail.

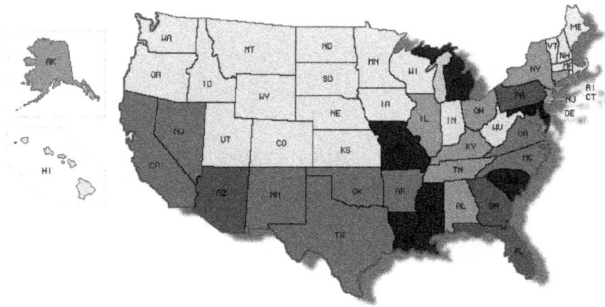

This is a map of the United States in 2011 covering gun homicide rates in all 50 states. The rate is derived by taking the total homicides committed with a firearm in each state and dividing by that state's total population. The data comes from the FBI which, in turn, gets the data from most, but not all law enforcement agencies within each state. This information is awaited eagerly by all criminologists, public health researchers, law enforcement bureaucrats and anyone else who makes a living or (like me) just enjoys thinking about crime. Why? Because once the data appears, everyone can then play the Great American Crime Game.

I'm actually thinking of going to one of the on-line game companies, like MassDiGi or IGP, and talking to them about creating an online version of this game, because internet gaming revenues are going to exceed \$35 billion this year (2014) so why shouldn't I get onto the gravy train? Anyway, here's how the game works: you choose a particular category of what the FBI calls "index" crimes, like murder, or robbery, or assault. Then you click the button that says, "Create a list" and the game gives you the rate for that crime in all 50 states. Then you click a button that says, "Create an average," and the game gives you five groupings of states: well above average, above average, average, below average and way below average. Then you choose a shade for each group (I chose dark for way above average to light for way below) and click 'Make map' and you get a map like the one above, which I created by doing exactly what I just described.

Now here's where it gets interesting. Once you have your map based on state-level crime rates of a particular index crime, you are then allowed to choose another variable of state-level data from any one of the following groups: economic, demographic, social and criminal. In the economic group, for instance, you can choose per capita or family income, employment and so forth. From the demographic group you can pull data that covers race, religion, home ownership, etc. The social data might let you use such criteria as educational levels, type of employment, etc., etc., etc. Believe me when I tell you that between the Census, the CDC and the UCR, there's enough state-level data to keep the game going forever.

How do you win the Great American Crime Game? It's simple. Create a map in which the colors for some other type of data looks just like the map we've created for violent crime, in particular homicides with guns or, if that's not possible, then aggravated assaults either with our without guns. The game goes on until a player comes up with a really exact match between those violent crimes and some other demographic or economic data that would allow us to explain, from the perspective of gun violence, why light is light, dark is dark, and everything in between is shaded in between.

Here's two maps that I created using state-level crime data. Map #2 gives statewide data for aggravated assaults.

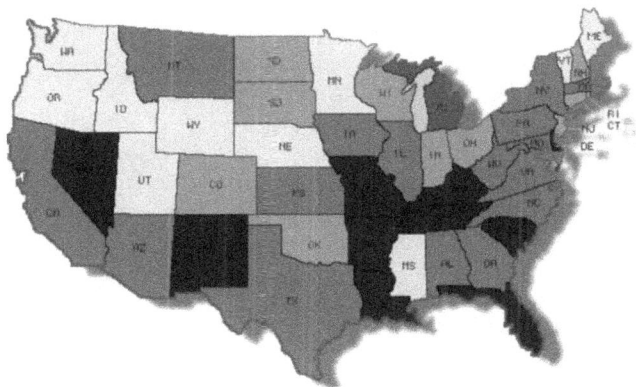

Map 2 – Aggravated Assault Rate

Now compare this map to Map #1 on statewide gun homicides (data from Illinois had not yet been received by the time the FBI published its 2012 Uniform Crime Report). Notice that the big, light (way below average) swatch of Western states in Map 1 has changed, and so has the concentration of dark (way above average) states in the Southeast. What the game is now showing us is that the Northeast has become less dangerous for aggravated (serious) assaults versus homicides, whereas more of the South and the Southwest have become more dangerous in terms of serious assault-types of crime.

Now let's make the game show us another map based on statewide, aggravated assaults with a gun:

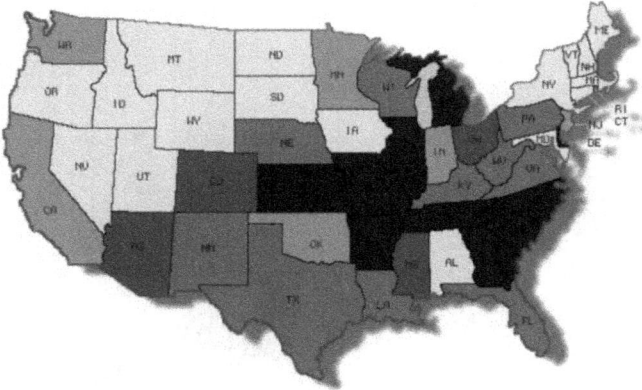

Map 3

All of a sudden, if we compare Maps 2 and 3, we're moving back to where we were in Map 1: the way below average aggravated assault with guns is more obvious throughout the West, the way above average is more concentrated in the Southeast. But before we go beyond the maps that we have created through crime data, we need to spend a bit of time explaining the ins and outs of the crime data itself. I know, I know, I promised not to bore you with data. Believe me when I tell you that all you're getting is the tip of the iceberg, so be content with that.

The FBI's Uniform Crime Reports are made up of what they call "index" crimes, which are the crime categories which they believe are both the most important and the ones that are easiest to compare on a state-by-state basis, homicide being the easiest of all. Where things get a little tricky is separating out various degrees of serious crime, as well as trying to distinguish degrees of criminal activity in an incident in which more than one crime took place. Finally, there's also the issue of what to include in the various categories, which is somewhat like picking companies for the Dow Jones market report. You can't choose too many companies or things get unwieldy; on the other hand you want the Dow Jones to be representative of the economy as a whole and you want to use companies whose financials and other business reports can really be trusted to be true. The same considerations come into play when trying to map out crime.

The FBI uses eight crime categories to create its Uniform Crime Reports: violent crimes, which are homicide, rape, robbery and aggravated assault, and property crimes, which are burglary, larceny over $50, arson and motor vehicle theft. Arson was added to the UCR in 1978, the other categories comprised the report since it was first issued in 1930. The FBI claims that the report rolls up to represent the law enforcement agencies which together cover 95% of the country's total population. And because the same agencies report year after year, not only is the report representative of trends over time, but it is also accurate both in terms of the number of crimes and the rate of crimes in each state. That's the reason that our little crime game can be so much fun, because according to the FBI, we can assume that what we are looking at is true.

Except for one little thing. I don't know if you've noticed, but whenever I present or summarize evidence, there always seems to be one little thing. And the one little thing in this case is the fact that the entire UCR is based on what the cops tell the FBI. And what the cops tell the FBI is based, in large part, on what people tell the cops. And since there's another agency that issues an annual report on what people both tell the cops and don't tell the cops, we also need to look at what that report says about crime. And those numbers are somewhat different.

What I'm talking about is the Department of Justice's National Crime Victimization Survey that is published annually by the Bureau of Justice Statistics, which is the record-keeping arm of the DOJ. I'm somewhat impressed by the methodology employed by the BJS because, if nothing else, they really do talk to a lot of folks about whether they have been victims of crime. In fact they divide the whole country into what they call Primary Sampling Units, or PSU's, comprising 110 individual counties, groups of counties and large metropolitan areas, from which they choose around 40,000 households from which, in total, they interview more than 70,000 subjects at least twice each year.

That's a pretty significant sample, far beyond anything I have ever seen from Gallup, Pew, or the other polling companies whose surveys regularly inform television viewers about how Americans feel about this and that. Now let's look at the survey in a little more detail. The questionnaire utilized for the 2012 survey contained 160 questions that cover the identity and demographics of the persons being questioned, followed by a large group of questions about the crime and the victimization itself, then followed by the following questions beginning with #116: "How did the police find out about it?" And then the next question is: "What was the reason it was not reported to the police?"

The answers to these two questions mark the point at which the BJS Victimization Survey and the FBI's Uniform Crime Report diverge in a major way; a divergence, incidentally, that is mentioned almost in passing in the BJS Annual Report and, of course, isn't mentioned by the FBI at all. The good news is that the BJS, in addition to the summary report, also publishes more than 100 detailed tables covering every question in the survey and, if the Devil is usually in the details of all reports, in this case he's sitting there grinning at the top of every page. Let me explain what I mean, though I promise that in a bit we'll get back to constructing our maps and playing our game.

According to the FBI, there were 657,545 aggravated assaults committed in 2012. This is the evidence that we are using when we play the Great Crime Game. According to the BJS, however, there were 996,110 aggravated assaults, or at least that's how many people they estimated to have been victims of aggravated assaults. In the overall findings, the BJS states that serious violent crimes (the index crimes) were underreported by 55%. If that's true, then this brings the FBI figure of 650,000+ into the neighborhood of the number published by the BJS. But let's drill down a little further, because it turns out that these global numbers hide some significant differences which may force us to re-think how we play our Great American Crime Game.

In all crimes of violence, or what the BJS calls "personal" (as opposed to "property") crimes, the degree of underreporting of crimes varies from one racial group to another. You're probably thinking that blacks tend to underreport crimes more than whites, right? Wrong. When it comes to all violent crimes, only 45% of white respondents reported the incident to the police, whereas nearly 60% of all black violent crimes were called in to the cops. The racial disparity is even more significant when we look at aggravated assaults, where serous assaults involving a weapon were reported only 49% of the time by whites and 76% of the time by blacks. When the assault involved an injury, the white reporting jumped to 72%, but it was 96% for African Americans who were injured in a serious assault.

What makes this racial difference between black and white reporting of serious assaults even more significant is the fact that the same people who report a higher percentage of these crimes, the black victims, are also more convinced that the police don't want to be bothered responding to their reports about crime. In the case of robbery, the difference isn't very great with 20% of blacks and 16% of whites believing that the cops will do something if they report this kind of crime. Yet when it comes to serious assaults, only 6% of whites believe that the police won't respond to their reports of this crime, whereas 13%—more than double—of blacks believe that serious assaults against them won't be taken seriously. Yet in the face of this more frequent belief that dealing with black victims of assaults won't get a response from the authorities, the black victims still report these crimes to a much greater degree than whites. I'm going to come back to this reporting issue from a much different perspective in Chapter 5, but for the meantime keep it in mind as we continue to play our crime game, while recalling that the last two maps were derived from statewide rates for aggravated assaults.

All right, now we're going to create another map. And this map will give us a state-by-state view of household income from our friends at the U.S. Census who compile something each year known as the American Community Survey Statistics, a.k.a. the ACS. You think the FBI or the BJS has data? Honey, you ain't seen nuthin' until you look at the ACS. Because we can find out just about everything that's going on in every state and we can drill down to counties and to cities and towns and even individual streets. But since, for the time being, our crime data is only being loaded into our game at the statewide level, we'll stick with statewide data from the ACS too.

Let's create a map of household incomes.

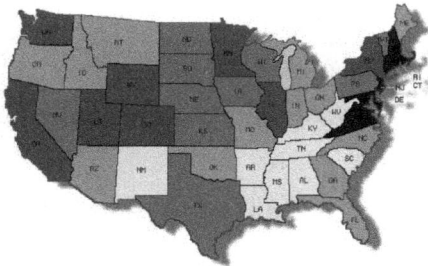

Map 4 – Household Income

Notice that the darker states (way above average) on this map tend to cluster within the Northeast just as they do in Map 3, but light shades completely disappear from the states out West. On the other hand, lighter states (way below average) for the most part remain light on both maps. Does this mean that there's a possible correlation between household income and aggravated assaults with guns, both in terms of higher income meaning less assaults and lower income meaning more? We can't really say that because the income-assault rate correlation completely disappears when we look towards the West. So the game has to go on, but don't worry. Plenty of data that we can use to create our maps lies ahead.

Let's plug race into the game. The next map shows the percentage of each state's total population that is comprised of African Americans.

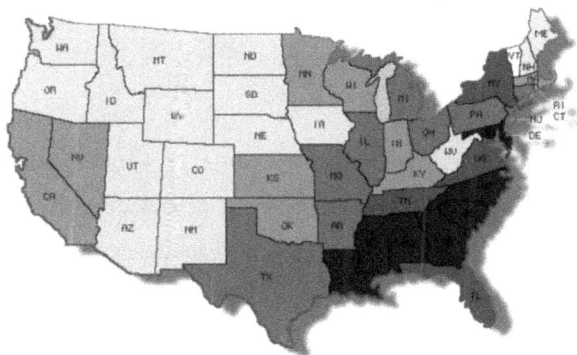

Map 5

Since I want the shades in all maps to be consistent, I have made light states way below average and darker states way above average for the proportion of African American residents living in each state. If, as the research indicates, African Americans suffer a disproportionate amount of violent crime, particularly violence involving guns, shouldn't this map, in which light states have a much smaller percentage of black residents than the dark states, look like Map 1 in which light states have almost no gun violence and dark states have an excessive amount? Let's bring back Map 1:

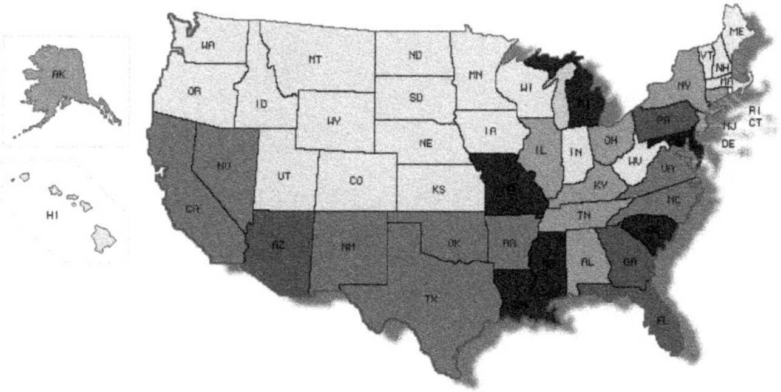

Map 1

Pretty close, wouldn't you say? Once again the Western states correlate pretty well between low rates of gun violence and low percentages of black residents. But we also know that the African-American population, or at least that part of the population which is associated with high violence rates, tends to be clustered primarily in urban locations. So does the comparison of Map 1 and Map 5 take that into account? Let's re-do our map again and this time plug in population density for each state:

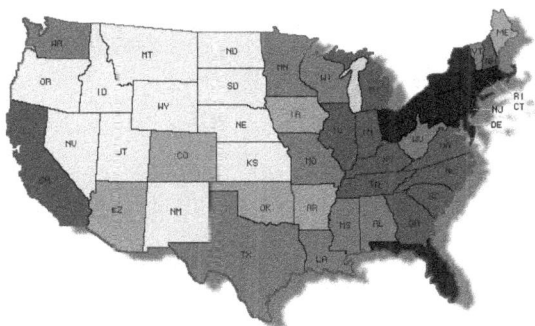

Map 6

Now the game changes again, because the lighter states that are below and way below average for population density more closely match the map showing percentages of black residents than the map showing state homicide rates. And this difference has to do not just with the location of the African-American population on a state-by-state basis, but the location of African Americans within each state. Because if you really want to understand where gun violence occurs, you have to look not at state-level data, but at data from what the Office of Management and Budget refers to as Metropolitan Statistical Areas, or MSA's.

According to the OMB, the United States currently contains 381 MSAs which are defined as areas with an urban core of at least 50,000, as well as an adjacent region whose population has close ties to the urban core due to work commuting, economic activities and so forth. The 2010 census lists the top 10 MSAs as being: New York, Los Angeles, Chicago, Dallas-Fort Worth, Houston, Philadelphia, Washington, D.C., Miami, Atlanta and Boston. Together these 10 metro sprawls contained roughly 77 million people in 2010, or 25% of the entire U.S. population. The next 10 largest MSAs contained another 36 million, for a total of roughly one-third of all U.S. residents. The total homicide count for these 20 largest MSAs was roughly 7,000, or half the total U.S. homicides reported that year by the FBI. If I were to include the 10 next largest MSAs, which would increase the MSA population to 125 million, or about 40% of the entire U.S. population, the homicide number climbs over 8,000, which is almost 60%.

The CDC calculated firearm homicides in the 50 largest MSAs, but they compiled the data for two years combined, 2009 and 2010, so I cannot compare it exactly to the overall murders that occurred in the largest 30 MSAs in 2010. Nevertheless, the urban nature of gun homicide is also evident in the CDC study, because they found that 66% of all gun homicides recorded in 2009-2010 were committed in the fifty largest MSAs, whose total population was about half of the U.S. national population. If you glance back at the map on population densities, you'll notice that only one of the 30 largest MSAs (Denver) is located in a state whose population density is less than the national average.

But even bringing the analysis down to the MSA level can hide some important evidence about gun violence. For example, the city with the highest gun homicide rate for African Americans is not Chicago, not New Orleans, not Philadelphia, not any of the cities whose cores serve as the center of MSAs with overall higher-than-average violent crime rates. The *numero uno* killing spot for African Americans is currently Omaha, the home town of America's most successful investor, Warren Buffet, but also a city whose murder rate for African Americans in 2013 topped 34 per 100,000 and made Nebraska the state with the highest black murder rate of all 50 states! This homicide rate, incidentally, represented a total of 27 actual black homicide victims, a far cry from the 500+ in Chicago or the 600+ in Detroit. But the murder rate in Omaha meant that you were five times more likely to get killed if you lived in Omaha than if you lived in the Windy City. This may be the home that Warren Buffet purchased in 1958 and in which he still resides, but I'll bet it's not even walking distance to where any of those 27 murders in Omaha took place.

We will never understand why 27 Black men got shot in Omaha by looking at data that in any way captures anything having to do with Warren Buffet. He may live in the same city as these 27 unfortunate victims, but he has absolutely nothing to do with them and they have absolutely nothing to do with him. The odds of Warren Buffet getting hit with the bullet from the barrel of a gun are about the same as the odds of Warren Buffet walking down the driveway of his home and being run over by a rhinoceros. And that's the problem with the Great American Crime Game; it still doesn't explain why some people just need to pull out and use a gun.

Let's play one more round of our Great American Crime game to try and find some kind of data that correlates with the information we have on where people use guns. Here's Map 1 again which is gun violence state-by-state:

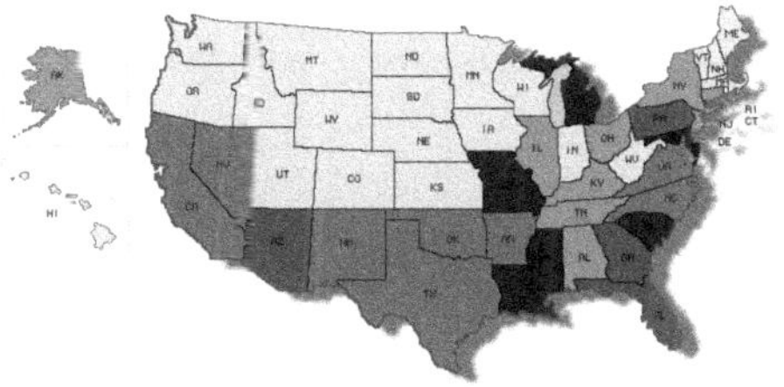

Map 1

Now here's a map which gets pretty close to state rates that are similar to rates for gun violence:

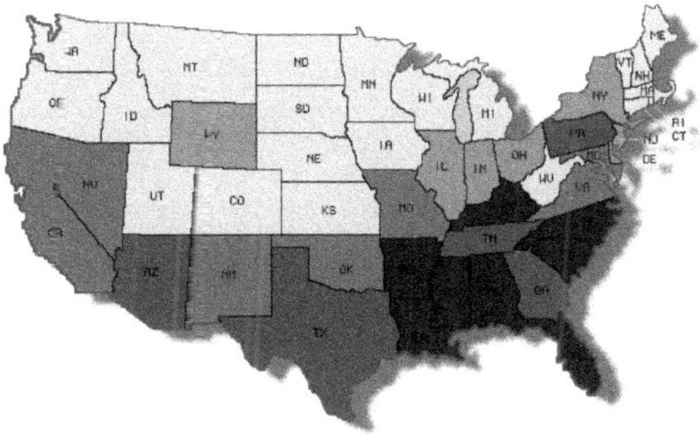

Map 7

The data for Map 7 came from the National Barbeque Association, which is the trade group that promotes eating barbeque all over the United States. And they provided me with a list of what they believe to be the per-capita consumption of barbeque in every state. Know what? With a couple of exceptions, the biggest being Texas which moves from average for gun violence to above average for eating barbeque, it's a pretty good fit. The point of this slightly tongue-in-cheek comparison is that after all the data and all the research, we still don't know why some people pull out a gun and use it but a lot of people don't.

Which carries us right into the next issue, namely, if we have lots of people walking around with guns and yet most people don't use them against themselves or other people, is there something about the United States which is different from other countries where people don't use guns against themselves or others because they don't have guns? This is another one of those "elephant in the living room" questions that hangs over every argument about guns. We have lots more guns per capita floating around than any other advanced country, there's a chart at the beginning of Chapter 6 that proves this beyond a shadow of a doubt. We also have a much higher gun homicide rate and homicide in general than any other advanced country (see the chart in Chapter 6), and while you can't say that there's an exact causal relationship between a) the existence of guns and b) the use of guns for any and all purposes, it's pretty tough to deny that a doesn't lead to b. But the total population of the other OECD countries isn't even twice the total population of the United States, and together the U.S. and OECD population is less than 15% of the global numbers as a whole Plus, while the United States alone counts for only 5% of the world's population, our so-called elevated homicide rate is only 3% of the homicides recorded throughout the globe. Even though we own roughly one-third of all the civilian guns. What's going on?

To understand this whole issue better we have to take a look at a remarkable document produced in 2011 by the UN. It's called *2011 Global Study on Homicide*, produced by the United Nations Office on Drugs and Crime, and it is without doubt the single most impressive resource on guns and gun violence that I have ever read. Until I read this report, I tended to resist comparisons about violence and gun violence between the United States and most other countries, if only because I am always reluctant, in trans-national comparisons, to assume that what means something in one country means anything remotely close to the same thing somewhere else. I have always assumed that differences in history, culture, development and the myriad other factors that go into creating every country were simply too great to brush aside in a search to discover some transcendent commonalities that might explain what cannot be understood just by looking at one country by itself. But the aggregation and analysis of worldwide data is so comprehensive in this report that it's the similarities, rather than the differences between such varied countries and regions that over and over again seems to stand out. Here's a couple of examples:

In 2010 the global homicide rate stood at 6.9 per 100,000 inhabitants, which is above the 2010 U.S. rate of 4.7, but that's if you use the data from the FBI-UCR. If you use the data from the CDC, our rate is 5.4. The U.N. actually gives data on homicide both from criminal justice and public health sources for just about every country under review, and it is interesting to note that public health estimations of homicide rates are higher than rates computed by law enforcement in most countries around the globe. The only countries that present lower public health homicide numbers than law enforcement numbers are most of the other countries in the OECD. Once we look beyond Europe, we discover that the disparity between public health and police measurement of homicide that we find in the United States is found in other non-OECD countries as well.

In addition to the differences in public health versus law enforcement measurement of homicide that we seem to share with less-developed countries, we also share an elevated homicide rate with fewer countries that report elevated rates, even though most of these high-violence countries are much less developed economically than we are. Of the 207 countries captured in this U.N. report, only 73 had homicide rates equal or higher than the U.S. rate, while 133, or two-thirds, registered lower homicide rates. The latter group includes virtually all the other OECD countries, but it also includes most of the Middle East, such as Israel, Kuwait, Lebanon, Saudi Arabia, Yemen, and virtually all of Asia, particularly the Indian sub-continent (with the exception of Pakistan) and adjacent regions. And while the data points towards a rough correlation between elevated homicide and lack of economic development, the report is careful to point out that low levels of economic development do not necessarily explain all instances of elevated homicide when such factors as the activity of drug cartels in highly-developed Latin American zones are taken into account.

Where U.S. and non-U.S. murder activity tends to show the strongest similarities, however, is the degree to which our homicides are primarily a function of the specific space in which they occur, namely, within urban areas and, generally speaking, within the most disadvantaged neighborhoods within those urban areas. For example, here is a map of South Africa's Capetown with homicide rates for each police precinct, the darkest precincts having rates above 42 per 100,000:

The precincts identified above—Khayelitsha, Nyanga and Guguletu—accounted for nearly half the homicides recorded in the entire city, and they are also three of the most economically depressed neighborhoods in all of Capetown. Now let's compare Capetown to New York:

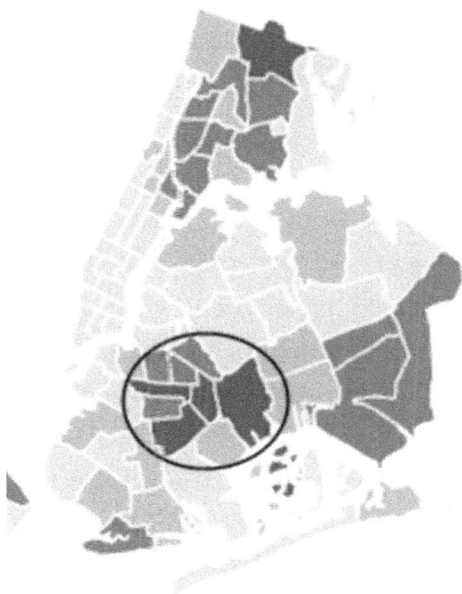

The areas of the New York map identified above registered the highest homicide rates in 2010 and are also the most economically depressed neighborhoods in New York City. I will discuss New York crime and violence in detail in Chapter 6, but the point to be made here is that while America's national homicide rate is far below the rate registered in South Africa (5.6 to 33.8 respectively,) the *pattern* of homicide in both countries is very similar, regardless of differences in overall economic and social development. There are, in fact, neighborhoods in

Capetown whose homicide rates are as low as rates experienced in the wealthiest parts of New York, another similarity of violence and violent behavior that blurs rather than enhances trans-national differences.

It should be clear to the reader that in trying to understand gun violence, the moment we begin to aggregate data about anything related to what we believe to be factors that might explain its occurrence, we lose the ability to understand why gun violence exists at all. Because even if we find similarities between social-economic circumstances in a high-violence area in a highly developed country like the United States versus a high-violence area in a less developed country like South Africa, we still do not know why *this* individual pulls out a gun and bangs away, whereas *that* individual does not. And the anomalies become even more difficult to explain when we drill down deeper into the data, for example, the fact that advanced countries like Norway and Hungary have gun homicide rates that are a fraction of the U.S. rate, but have percentages of female victims of homicide that are more than twice as high.

One other point about comparing gun violence from place to place. We noted above that the international homicide rate is somewhere around 7. But it's not the case that people commit the same amount of violence no matter where we look. In fact, the overall rate is basically a function of homicide rates in two areas of the globe—middle Africa on the one hand and Central/Latin America and the Caribbean on the other. If we pull the countries with the above-average highest homicide from these two zones out of the 207 countries that comprised the U.N. survey in 2010, the homicide rate for the remaining 147 countries drops to less than 2. If we pull black and Hispanic homicides out of the total American homicide count, then our homicide rate drops to less than two. It's not easy to sustain the argument (even though I have seen it on some crazy right-wing blogs) that our current level of violence is due to all these immigrants bringing this type of behavior with them when they (illegally) land on our shores, particularly since the bulk of our homicides involve African Americans who last arrived here as "immigrants" fifty years before the Civil War. But the 60 countries where most homicide occurs throughout the world also include the countries with the lowest levels of economic growth and the highest levels of poverty and social dislocation for which violence is not just a symptom, but probably also a disease. Why should it be any different here?

How do we figure this whole violence thing out? How do we understand what really makes someone—

anyone—behave violently, and not just behave violently but behave violently to the point that out comes the gun? I have gone about as far as I can go by giving you answers to these questions through aggregating and analyzing data and I don't think the answers get us very far. So in the last two chapters I'm going to reverse things and look not at the environments and instances where gun violence takes place, but try instead to figure out the behavior of who the cops refer to as the "doers" themselves.

CHAPTER 5

DID I REALLY PULL THE TRIGGER?

Now that we are finally going to try and figure out why something happens that we call gun violence, let's begin the discussion by recalling how many acts of gun violence really occur. And the reason we are going to summarize this information is because if you have read this far in the book you'll notice that most of the numbers cover the number of victims of gun violence and in this chapter we are finally getting to the people whose behavior results in gun violence taking place.

Every year there are around 11,000 gun homicides, 19,000 suicides, slightly less than 1,000 accidental gun deaths and another 50,000-75,000 gun injuries, the ratio of killed to wounded being a function of the proficiency of the people who shoot the guns. We can assume pretty much that the ratio of perpetrators to victims in gun deaths (homicides, suicides, accidents) is probably pretty close to 1:1. As for the injuries, that's a little trickier, particularly since we don't have very good data on exactly how many guns ended up being used in assaults. According to the FBI, one out of every five serious assaults is carried out with a gun. But the data from the National Crime Victim Survey raises gun victimizations to well above 400,000. And neither of these sources give us a count on whether each of these assaults was carried out by a unique attacker, or whether the assaults ended up in wounds resulting from a gun trigger actually being pulled.

If we put all the data together, however, and try to look at the issue in the most modest terms, we can say with some degree of certainty that each year there are at least a quarter of a million people who at one point or another pulled out a gun and held it in their hands while it went—bang! I'm not saying this is an accurate number, but the accurate number isn't the issue here. We know where these people live, we know where they use the guns and we know why they use the guns. The answer to the unanswered question of what makes them commit gun violence isn't going to change just because we decide that there are more or less of them than what the official numbers say. Whatever the real number, the fact is that there are millions of people walking around with guns and many millions more who own guns and almost none of either group do what this particular group, the shooters, do with their guns. You have now read more than 30,000 words of this book and we still don't know what makes this group do what it does. And believe me, if we knew, I would have already given you the answer.

To start, let's go back to the issue that we first discussed at the very beginning of the book, namely, the issue of violence. What is violence? It is behavior that results in harm. And the behavior may be impulsive and engaged in without thought, or it may be planned but either way, the result is harm. And how do we know that harm has occurred? Because someone is damaged. The damage doesn't have to be physical but an individual or a group of individuals cannot be the victims of violence unless they can show some palpable degree of damage to themselves, their psyches or to someone under their care. No damage, no harm. No harm, no violence. So let's start with the most obvious way in which people can use guns to commit harm, and in this case we are talking about suicide, which is a very obvious and simple way to do great harm to yourself. Particularly if you use a gun.

But the first problem with suicide involving guns is that it's not a crime to shoot yourself. And this gets back to the whole notion of violence, namely, that someone has to damage somebody else and therefore be made to compensate the victim who suffered an injury in some fashion or another. But the guy who just blew his own brains out isn't in much of a position to do anything to compensate himself for the injury he just suffered, so even if there's a dead body resulting from unnatural circumstances, there hasn't been a crime.

Not only isn't suicide a crime, it's also a personal or family thing. And since nobody will be charged with doing anything wrong, why draw attention to the reasons for the death unless the reasons have to be known? Consequently, coroners and medical examiners aren't as careful about listing suicide as a cause of death as they might be when it comes to a homicide, particularly a homicide with a gun. We don't have exact numbers on this issue, but it appears to be possible that the underreporting of suicides ranges in different Western countries and localities to be anywhere between 15 and 40 percent. It is probably the case that underreporting of gun suicides is less likely than other types of methods, but the bottom line is that the annual number of U.S. suicides, which is roughly 38,000+, is no doubt a minimum figure and would probably be somewhere in the mid-40 thousands if the real numbers could ever be found.

The last year for which we have aggregate national numbers for suicide is 2010, and in that year, according to the CDC, more than 38,000 American committed suicide, half of whom used guns. A majority of these poor unfortunates were white males between 35 and 60 who live primarily in small and smaller towns in Western states. That's right: the population that is most prone to using gun violence against themselves live for the most part in the states which have the lowest percentage of people who use a gun against someone else. Don't believe me? Just compare the map below which is shaded by statewide firearm suicide rates with the map on the next page that captures state gun violence rates:

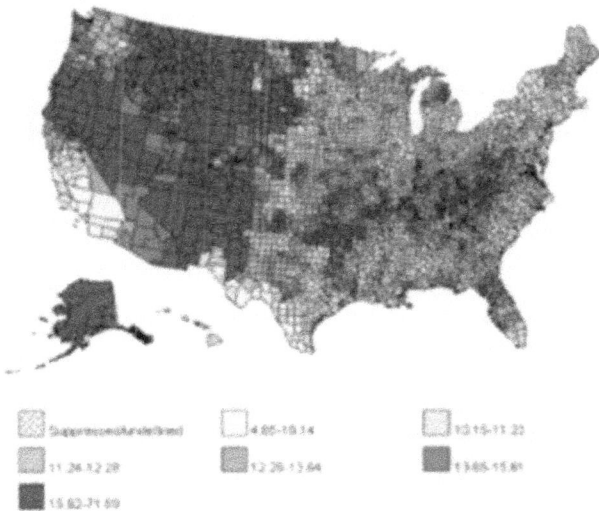

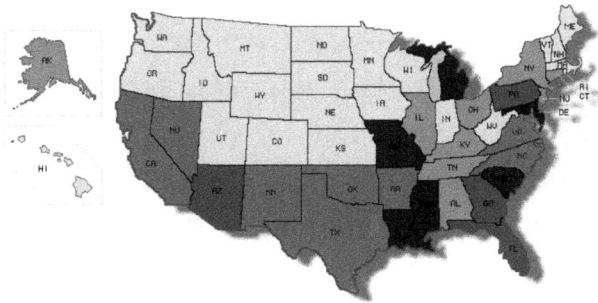

Sorry, the shades are different because the suicide map comes from the CDC, not from me. But notice where the greatest concentration of high-rate suicide counties are located: exactly in the same areas that have little, if any gun homicides. These are also the states that have the highest per-capita ownership of guns, numbers which we have to estimate based on NICS background checks recorded by the FBI. I discuss the limitations of NICS data in detail in Volume 1, so I'll spare you the bother of going over those comments again. But let's just say that although we can't give precise information on state-by-state gun ownership from NICS data or anything else, the comparative value of NICS for understanding patterns and location of gun ownership is fairly strong. What we do know is that there has been enough research over the years to validate the idea that the more guns you have lying around your home, the easier it will be to pull one out and use it to shoot yourself.[1]

So we don't think of states like Montana and North Dakota as being violent, right? That is absolutely true if you listen to the NRA. Because they can't wait to tell you, again and again, that gun violence has been going down over the last twenty years, and in fact it has declined by more than 50% since 1993. Which is all well and good if you define gun violence only in criminal terms. But if you include suicide as a type of gun violence, the number and the rate of gun suicides has not been going down since 1993, in fact it has been going up. So a state like Montana that is shaded light in the map of statewide gun violence because hardly anyone shoots anyone else with a gun, all of a sudden becomes average or above average for gun violence when the guys who shoot their guns at someone happen to be that someone themselves. And if there were significant numbers of people in these states who pointed the gun at themselves and pulled the trigger, how many more were there who, for one reason or another, thought about doing it, almost did it, but somehow stopped short? Are these people any less victims of gun violence than the owner of the little deli on the corner who finds himself staring into the muzzle of a gun that luckily didn't go off as he scooped some cash out of the register and gave it to the kid standing there and pointing the gun in his face?

I know a guy in his late 50s who used to be a cop. At some point while he was still on the job his wife dumped him, his kids grew up and moved away, and when he took his 20 and left the job he suddenly realized he was all alone. So he started drinking and got himself a part-time gig as a security guard at a state-run facility, which was enough hours to give him some extra cash but didn't interfere with the dozen or so tops that he popped sitting in front of the television every night. He was also a smoker, of course overweight, and one day he felt that he was having trouble breathing so he stopped at the clinic and, following some tests he learned that he had COPD. So he's sitting at home that night, he's fifty-nine years old, nobody really cares whether he's alive or dead, he can't stop smoking or drinking and even the food he used to enjoy doesn't taste all that good.

All of a sudden he noticed that his service revolver was sitting on the coffee table in front of the couch, he didn't remember putting it out there but it was within reach and it was loaded, ready to go bang. This is a completely true story, by the way. I didn't make it up. So this guy reaches for the gun, he's not consciously thinking about suicide but he's sitting there miserable on his couch and he's reaching for a loaded gun. And literally as he put his hand on the revolver there was a knock on his door, then the door swung open and a woman's voice called out, "Anyone home?" It was his neighbor who had taken a package for him earlier in the day and, having come home from her own job, wanted to make sure he got the delivery before she forgot and dumped it into the trash.

This friend of mine later realized that the totally coincidental intervention by his neighbor not only saved his life at that moment but pushed him into alcohol rehab and therapy, although he's taking things one day at a time so he still smokes and later he'll worry about the CCPD. I believe that my friend was as much a victim of gun violence as anyone else who ever finds themselves looking at a gun that could be used to inflict harm, whether someone else is the shooter or whether the person looking at the gun is thinking of pulling the trigger and aiming the gun at himself. It's a traumatic moment either way and, in the case of my friend, it was the fact that he escaped unharmed from the trauma that turned his life around. But let's not underestimate the psychic effect of reaching towards that gun.

It shouldn't come as a surprise that the states which counted the highest suicide rates also head up the list of states whose populations are more prone to thinking about committing suicide. In fact, of the 12 states with the highest percentage of residents who considered a suicide attempt, nine of them were located either in the Midwest or the West, and all of them have rates of gun ownership far above the national average. Together these states (OH, MO, IN, CO, AR, WY, ID, NV, UT) contain around 40 million people, of whom about 5 percent were suicide risks and I would suspect that gun ownership amongst this population was probably near universal if not one hundred percent.

I wish I could devise a more scientific method for determining how many suicide-prone individuals are perhaps more vulnerable because they happen to own a gun. Unfortunately, the only logical research method that could be employed would be to ask physicians or other health professionals dealing with these people to query them about their whether there are guns sitting around in their homes. But while the NRA has made endless noise about the reasons why physicians would be violating a patient's privacy by asking about the existence of guns, the fact is that in Western states like Montana, Utah and Idaho, along with rural Midwestern areas in Ohio and Indiana, there's really no sense in asking about guns because it's a pretty good assumption that the answer would always be "yes."

Ever hear of Skidmore, Missouri, a farming community of less than 400 residents located about 100 miles north of Kansas City in the tiny little corner of the state formed by the meandering of the Missouri River as it flows down between Nebraska and Iowa? The town's in the middle of nowhere and it's always been in the middle of nowhere, but in 1980 the town briefly caught the attention of the entire country a when a local bad-boy and bully names Ken McElroy was gunned down by "persons unknown" as he sat in his truck in the middle of town. McElroy, whose murder was turned into a best-selling book and a Grade-B movie that played in virtually every drive-in theater throughout the Midwest, had been convicted of shooting the local grocery-store owner but had appealed the conviction and was out on bond. Over the years he had been accused, but never convicted, of an endless series of violent crimes, and when the town residents saw him first drinking in the town saloon and then sitting in his pickup with his rifle on the back rack, a quick meeting was held down the street, more than 50 residents gathered in sight of his vehicle and he was very quickly shot dead.

The case was investigated by the local chief, by the state police and ultimately by the FBI. Two grand juries were convened, virtually everyone in the town was forced to testify at one point or another, and the

Mafia should have as good a system for keeping everyone from saying a word. Forensic evidence was available (shell casings on the ground, bullets in the victim's chest and head), witnesses had lined up on both sides of the street, but nobody saw anything and no murder weapon was ever found. The investigation seemed to indicate that the shots that were fired at McElroy were at ranges of fifty to one hundred yards. Which was exactly the problem, because there wasn't a single man and probably very few women in Skidmore who couldn't hit a target the size of a man's head at that distance or even further away. And how many rifles in the caliber that killed McElroy were owned by residents of the town? Probably as many as there were people who could shoot such a gun, which means everyone who was around the little farming village that day.

To go back to our numbers, if we assume that 5% of the 40 million people who live in the states which have the highest rates of contemplated suicide spent some time in the last year thinking about taking their own lives, then we have to assume that virtually every single one of these individuals would have had little difficulty getting their hands on a gun. So if we are going to define gun violence not just as moments when a gun actually goes off, but also including moments when someone is confronted with the presence of a gun, then it's reasonable to add another several million potential suicide victims to the half million who report being victims of gun violence because a gun is held, but not used in someone's hand. If we are trying to figure out why some people pull the trigger and others don't, the size of the group that hasn't crossed the line from passive to active behavior just got much larger. All the more reason why we need to figure out why some people cross that line even though most do not.

In the case of suicides, where both the numbers and the motives are even more difficult to acquire or assess, we also find an anomaly as regards the use of guns. Overall, there has been a dramatic increase in suicides, particularly among men in their 50s, a rate which has jumped nearly 50 percent since 1999. But while shootings are still the most common form of life-ending behavior, the rate of gun use in suicides has increased more slowly than the use of other life-ending "mechanisms" (as the CDC euphemistically refers to the way people kill themselves), with gun suicides increasing by 14% while poisonings have increased by 25% and hangings up by over 80%.

Would suicide among adults occur less frequently if there were less guns in private homes? This is a contention of the gun control lobby and it's been batted back and forth between them and the NRA too many times to count. The suicide data collected carefully by the CDC might help shed some light on this issue, so here it is:

% gun suicides

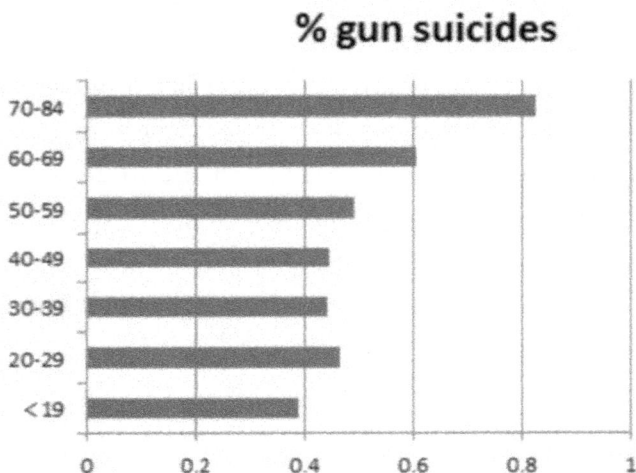

This chart is based on CDC data for 2010 taken from the Web-based Injury and Reporting System, aka WISQARS. It covers 37,382 of the 38,364 suicides reported that year, so it's more or less complete. What I have done is grouped victims by age groups (the vertical numbers) and by the percentage of suicides for which a gun was the way in which the suicide was carried out. The disparity between the numbers charted here and the overall suicide number (roughly 1,000) is due primarily to the fact that I did not include suicides in which the age was not known. Finally, of all suicide victims under the age of 19, more than 80% were ages 15 through 19, and while teen suicide has been increasing, it is still largely a behavior found in late teens.

Note that for all age groups until age 60, the percentage of suicides in which the instrument was a gun is fairly constant; i.e., between 38 and 48 percent. Then it jumps substantially, up to 60 percent for persons on the 60-69 age bracket and above 80 percent for individuals 70 years old and above (up to 84). And while the raw number of suicides in this group (3,328) is less than half the raw number for the age group 50-59 (8,187), the rate of firearm use based on the total U.S. population in that age cohort is more than 10% higher for the older age group.

What this chart and the data behind it clearly shows us is that while guns are the most frequent mechanism for suicide in all age groups beyond the teen years, the link between suicide and guns becomes stronger as the age of the suicide victim climbs higher. And it isn't just a slight increase in gun-related suicides as we move up the age scale, it's a very substantial increase and one that, as far as I can tell, has not been discussed in any detail in the literature on suicide, or gun violence or anything else. So in the absence of any research on this issue, I am going to go out on a limb and posit a kind of reverse connection between suicide gun violence and impulsive behavior, if only because suicide, as opposed to other forms of gun violence, does represent a direct and immediate link between what a gun can do and the reason for which it is being used.

Recall that I said in Chapter 3 that Zimring's research on the number of shots fired in gun assaults indicated a disconnect between the motives or desires of the shooter and the results of the act of shooting itself; namely, that since the overwhelming majority of fatal shootings involved only one discharge of the gun, that the shooter was motivated more by using the weapon than what was believed to be the end result. But the whole point about suicide is that since the shooter is aiming the gun at himself (or at herself in 20 percent of suicide deaths), the gun is only going off one time in virtually all cases, and in 95% of gun suicide attempts, that's all it takes. A study in Australia of more than 260 suicide notes found that the one reason found most frequently in older victims and hardly mentioned amongst younger suicides was the desire to escape from physical pain. What we are clearly talking about in older suicides is an end-of-life decision which in many cases simply hastens what would otherwise be a natural ending of one's life without the necessity to first endure more pain. Doctor Kevorkian and other physician-assisted suicide specialists would arrive at the bedside of a patient with some kind of contraption that had to be hooked up, twisted around the face or stuck into an extremity when, in fact, all he needed to use was a little thirty-eight.

I suspect that elderly people who commit suicide do so, in many cases, in order to spare themselves additional physical suffering over the last few months of their lives. I also suspect, incidentally, that many such incidents are not reported officially as suicides for reasons having to do with privacy, insurance and the fact that it's pretty easy for the coroner or cops to figure out that the individual died at their own hand. But I also suspect that it's only for the most part this senior age cohort of suicides who act consciously, carefully and without the impulsive motives or methods that characterize suicide in younger age groups.

It should be added that the United States is the only OECD country in which guns are the preferred method of what the CDC clinically refers to as the mechanism for ending one's own life. In other countries jumping, hanging oneself and poison (meaning overdoses) are the way people usually move from this life to the next. Yet even though Americans are the only OECD population to use guns in suicide more than 50% of the time (the next highest is Switzerland at 33%, with all other countries at or below 20% for gun use in suicide), our overall suicide rate of 10.1 per 100,000 puts us on a par with Canada, Germany and Norway, and below Denmark, Sweden and France. Would our suicide rate be even lower if so many of us didn't have such easy access to guns? The CDC's Second Injury Control and Risk Survey conducted 2001-2003 indicates that gun owners showed no greater amount of suicidal thoughts, but for those who did develop a suicide plan out of those thoughts, more than one in five said they planned to use a gun.

This is an important finding, because researchers who looked at possible links between suicide rates and gun ownership have been able to determine that states with higher levels of gun ownership also had higher suicide rates. And this finding holds true not just for the Western states, but is found in other parts of the country where gun ownership is not as prevalent as it is in the West.[1] Which brings us back to what I said about gun violence when I started this whole book, namely, the issue of impulse as the primary explanation for the violent use of guns.

Until now in this chapter we have assumed that gun violence occurs because someone is holding a gun and makes a conscious decision to pull the trigger. But what if the decision isn't conscious? What if the individual with the gun just forgets that it's loaded, or picks it up in an awkward fashion and accidentally or mistakenly pulls the trigger, whether or not this was the intention? According to the CDC, less than 1,000 gun homicides each year are ruled to be accidental shootings; in other words, whatever the person holding the gun was doing, he or she didn't intend to use it to commit an act of violence. Maybe they meant to threaten someone with violence but that was not their intention, at least not their conscious intention.

This blurring of the line between a conscious and unconscious act of gun violence takes place both with suicides and homicides. In the case of suicides, the issue is the extent to which suicide victims are also under the influence of alcohol or drugs at the time of their attempt to the point that they are only vaguely aware of what they are doing and do not necessarily imagine that their life is about to come to an end. A major study in 2012 concluded that nearly 25% of all adult suicide victims were legally intoxicated at their time of death, and these individuals were more likely to use violent means, such as shooting or choking themselves. So let's add this group to the 1,000 or so who kill someone accidentally. But this category has another, larger component as well.

Why is it that most people who feel depressed, even seriously depressed, resist the idea of ending their own lives? Why is it that most people who get into disagreements or arguments with other people leave their hands in their pockets and would never consider pulling out a gun? We can put together all the behavioral profiles we want that would capture virtually all the background information about people who are most likely to pick up a gun and use it to end their or someone else's life. In the case of suicide it's a white male, living in a smallish town, age 30-55 with a drinking problem, or a financial problem, or a marital problem or a combination of all three. In the case of homicide it's a black or Hispanic male, ages 16-35, living in an inner-city neighborhood, usually a drop-out from school and with a record of prior criminal activity usually involving non-lethal forms of violence but serious enough to attract the attention of police. So those are the people who, generally speaking, end up using a gun to take someone's life, whether it's their own life or the life of somebody else. The only problem is that for every individual who fits one of those two profiles there are tens, hundreds, thousands of people who fit the same profile and never use or perhaps even possess a gun. How do we figure out why most people don't feel it necessary to use a gun, which is ultimately the same issue as trying to figure out why a few of them do?

I am referring to the fact that we really have no idea how many homicides were consciously intended as opposed to shootings in which a perpetrator cannot be identified and the authorities have no choice but to designate the event as a homicide, because nobody is standing next to the victim saying, "duhhhh, I didn't know it was loaded." While the percentage of arrests for homicide are the highest for all four categories of violent crime (see below,) one out of every 4 homicides remains uncleared:

- Crime% arrested

- Homicide 75%

- Forcible rape 22%

- Robbery 30%

- Aggravated assault 55%

These numbers have been fairly consistent over the past ten years, and while murders are obviously the highest priority from a crime-solving point of view, this still leaves a bunch of people walking around who pulled out a gun and shot someone else for reasons that are not known or are certainly not clear. So here is where I am going to update the data in Chapter 3 that was studied by Frank Zimring, because I have been able to look at data covering more than 2,000 fatal shootings that occurred in various parts of the United States in 2010. The data is found in a remarkable CDC archive known as the National Violent Death Reporting System, and its use is subject to very rigorous guidelines to safeguard confidentiality, so I am going to have to generalize far beyond the specifics that Zimring was able to attach to his data derived from Chicago in 1970-72. Notwithstanding these constraints, the 2010 data indicates that more than 50% of the gun homicides resulted from a single discharge of a gun. Moreover, while 50% of the guns used in Zimring's research were small-caliber pistols or revolvers (.22 and .25 calibers), the NVDRS data covering 900+ gun homicides indicates that small-caliber weapons were utilized slightly more than 15% of the time, while more lethal calibers (38, 9mm, 40 and 45) were employed in almost 85% of the gun murders in which a handgun was used.[2]

These findings are not substantially different from what Frank Zimring found when he analyzed homicide data in Chicago from 1970 and published his findings which we summarized in Chapter 3. And just to repeat his analysis, the fact that most deadly shootings occurred with only one shot being fired seems to indicate that the shooter is more interested in acting out an impulse to pull the trigger than in making a tangible connection between firing the gun and the consequent results. Because if the motivation behind gun use was to use the gun in its most efficient and practical way—to inflict great damage on the target—then it might be assumed that the shooter would empty the gun into his target or at least deliver multiple shots to increase the degree of harm and therefore increase the odds that the individual being shot would wind up dead.

Zimring concluded in the 1970's that the lethality of firearm use was a function of lethality of caliber rather than intention of the shooter, and if it was true then, it would certainly be more true today. And this is because the evolution of firearm manufacturing technology over the last 40 years has resulted in the appearance of smaller and smaller guns that deliver more and more firepower. Which is the reason I spent time in Chapter 3 discussing the ins and outs of the 9mm cartridge, because this vaunted military round which was considered the most lethal type of pistol ammunition in the 1970's is now somewhere in the middle range of handgun lethality, having been surpassed, for example, by the S&W 40 caliber round, among others. And not only are the calibers much more powerful and therefore much more lethal (even if the victim is hit by only one shot that enters the body in a non-lethal zone), but the guns are the size of an Android phone, weigh less than a pound, and have finishes that are resistant to even high degrees if wear and tear. In short, perfect for the street. The guns that were floating around Chicago when Zimring published his study were made of steel, they were hand polished and hand fitted and were coated with finishing compounds that needed to be rubbed and piled after every use or they would quickly spot, rust and then break down. The handguns on the market today are made from polymer; they are impervious to rust and just like they used to say about Timex watches, they take a licking and keep on ticking.

The fact that modern guns can absorb lots of abuse and still function as they were designed to function makes them all the more prevalent in areas and among individuals who want to carry guns. And it also means that once someone—anyone—in the local crowd has a gun, it's kind of like a nuclear arms race at the street-corner level, everyone else better get one too because you don't show up to a gunfight and bring a knife. When asked by researchers why they first acquired guns (in the Lizotte study that I mentioned in Chapter 1), youths between 14 and 16 usually started carrying guns because they were responding to peer pressure rather than for anything having to do with a particular use for the gun. It's the "he's got one, I want one" syndrome which is probably the most typical response that any consumer makes to explain the acquisition of anything that he or she didn't have before. Which is all the more reason why we have to take impulse into account when we talk about why someone shot off a gun. And our final chapter will take a look at the issue of impulse in greater detail and suggest a reason why it may play a bigger role in violence and gun violence than we usually think.

Notes to Chapter 5

1. M. Miller, et. al., "Firearms and Suicide in the Northeast," Journal of Trauma and Acute Care

2. Care Surgery, 57, 3 (September, 2004) 626-632. This research group has published similar findings for other parts of the country.

3. NCDRS Restricted Access Data, Subset: Coroner/medical examiner information. I wish to thank Catherine Barber from Harvard University School of Public Health for help in securing this data and enduring my pestering and queries.

CHAPTER 6

AND DON'T THINK YOU HAVE TO BE AN ASSHOLE TO BE AN ASSHOLE

We have been spending most of this book looking at gun violence as an irrational, impulsive act committed by people who are irrational and/or impulsive. For the most part this means kids, or immature adults. Because the numbers are quite clear on the fact that by the time someone reaches their mid to late 30's, if they haven't tried to kill someone by that point in their life, they probably won't try at all. More than three-quarters of the people who commit gun violence, regardless of sex, race or location, are people between the ages of 16 and 35, even though this slice of the age pyramid represents less than 20% of the population as a whole.

There seems to be solid scientific evidence which points to the fact that until at least the late 20's, if not early 30's, physical maturation particularly among males occurs at a much faster pace than mental development. Physiologically, we can jump tall buildings at a single bound well before we understand that at the end of the jump is a concrete sidewalk that will smash us to smithereens. And although we have a much clearer understanding of the links between neurological development and impulsive behavior thanks to technology advances like MRI imaging, you can go back to Shakespeare's *The Winter's Tale* where he spells it right out: "there were no age between ten and three-and-twenty, or that youth would sleep out the rest; for there is nothing in the between but getting wenches with child, wronging the ancientry, stealing, fighting."

Now I'm afraid you are going to have to wait for Volume 4 of our little series for more on this subject, which is where I spell out the relationship between guns, toys and kids (and adults), but for the time being let's just say that until the end of adolescence and sometimes well into the early adult years, males in particular do not seem to do a very good job of balancing impulses with an understanding of what may happen if they do something. And in addition to being impulsive, adolescents and young adults (according to Erik Erikson) also suffer from identity deficits, which is a fancy way of saying that they are easily influenced by their peers and the behavior of people around them, so if he's got a gun I better get one too, even if I know it's the wrong thing to do.

But what if you're not fifteen or sixteen years old? What if you are a 45-year-old IT engineer with a responsible job, no prior history of violence or any other form of illegal behavior, and no possible justification for putting ten pistol rounds into a vehicle that was driving away from you without even the slightest possibility that the car's occupants were gearing up for an attack? This is what happened near Jacksonville, Florida on November 12, 2012 when Michael Dunn, the aforementioned software engineer, emptied his gun into a Dodge, Durango with three of the bullets hitting and killing a 19-year-old passenger named Jordan Davis whose provocative behavior seems to have consisted of the usual "fuck you" when Dunn told him and his buddies to turn down the "rap crap" that was blaring from the vehicle's radio.

Dunn is white and the dead kid was black. The jury actually deadlocked on whether Dunn felt threatened enough by Davis to justify pulling his gun and banging away at the kid. Maybe Davis got out of the Durango and maybe he didn't. Maybe he yelled some threats at Dunn and maybe he didn't. Remember we're talking about Florida, and where Davis was killed was less than a two-hour's drive from where Trayvon Martin was shot. But in this case there were plenty of witnesses, including Dunn's fiancée, whose versions of the incident didn't exactly exonerate Dunn, but what probably cooked his goose was that after the shooting Dunn got in his car, drove away, took his dog for a walk, ate a pizza, went to bed and didn't tell anyone about the incident until he was picked up by the cops the following day. He may have gotten off the murder charge but even a Florida jury couldn't overlook the fact that he kept shooting at a vehicle that was driving away, and that behavior could net him up to 60 years at Lake Butler and having been in Lake Butler I can tell you that the mosquitoes are very large and very fierce.

In his defense, Dunn claimed that he didn't report the incident because he didn't believe that anyone had been hit. I wasn't in the courtroom where Dunn testified in his own defense, but I can't imagine how he could have kept a straight face while making such a comment in open court. He fired ten shots at a vehicle that was close at hand but didn't think there was any problem leaving the scene? As I explained in Volume 2, the National Rifle Association has gone to great lengths to establish the idea that carrying a gun around is something that will make us all safe. And they have a series of courses about how to use guns to defend yourself, including a course that I have taught called *Personal Defense in the Home*.

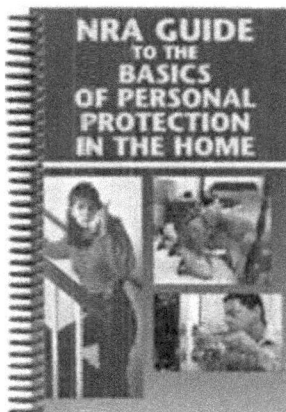

Actually, I spend most of this course talking about domestic violence, which the NRA would rather have you believe really doesn't exist. But to give the devil its due, at least the NRA recognizes the fact that if you pull out a gun and use it against someone else, a very big shit storm is going to erupt,

and you better be prepared to deal with it from a personal and legal point of view. And their advice in this respect is very sound. First and most important, and they repeat this numerous times, a gun should only be used in self-defense as an absolutely last resort, no ifs, ands, or buts. And if it is used in this way, whether you hit someone or not, you should immediately put down the gun, call 911, make a brief and clear statement about the shooting and then wait for the cops to come around. Period. End of story.

Dunn did none of those things, and I guarantee you that he was aware of these issues because in addition to being an IT engineer, he was also identified as a collector of guns. Which doesn't mean he necessarily owned a gun that was worth any real dough, because very few guns ever end up being worth the couple of hundred bucks that you paid for them. It probably means he liked going into gun stores, trading this one, buying that one, wandering through the aisles of a gun show, talking to fellow gun guys and, by the way, walking around in public with a gun. Before stopping at the convenience store where he encountered and then killed Jordan Davis, he had been in a very dangerous and threatening environment, one which certainly required him to take along his gun, namely the wedding reception of his son.

You may recall that back in Chapter 2 I discussed another shooting in Florida that took place in a movie theater outside of Tampa where a 71-year-old retired cop gunned down a 45-year-old businessman who was threatening him with a very dangerous weapon, to wit, a bag of popcorn. But what's so eerily interesting about both cases is that the cop in Tampa, Curtis Reeves, also violated all post-shooting rules of the NRA. He didn't separate himself from the gun, he didn't call 911 and he didn't even appear to be upset by the incident when the cops got to the scene. They even had to tussle with him to take away his gun.

But what I am going to tell you now is where these two shootings really meet. Because what I purposely left out of the recounting of the movie theater incident until now was the fact that at the time of the shooting, the theater in which both shooter and victim were sitting had less than 30 occupied seats! And at the time that Michael Dunn pulled out his Taurus 9mm pistol, he was standing in front of a convenience store and the Durango that was moving away from him was in the middle of a parking area that measured at least 600 square feet. In other words, and here is the real point of this section, this chapter and this entire book: two decent young men are dead because four people started arguing and impulse replaced any attempt to figure out rationally what needed to be done.

Don't think that the necessity to prove that you have the biggest swinging dick in the neighborhood is a particularly American phenomenon. It seems to hold true for everyone who has a swinging dick. By which I mean there seems to be a universal propensity on the part of male adolescents and even older adults to engage in impulsive behavior of all types, including violent impulsive behavior. And if they come from a background or environment in which violence is seen as normal, or useful, or just another run-of-the-mill type of behavior, then the inability of either party to back down becomes the stuff out of which violence will occur. And if anyone's carrying a gun, the violence may become gun violence.

But violence that may be typical adolescent behavior is one thing, gun violence is quite another. Because the problem with using a gun to express violence is the finality of its result. If the victim is lucky, his attacker doesn't know much about shooting guns and misses his mark. If the shooter knows what he's doing, the only reason you end up getting wounded instead of dead is because the shooter should have practiced more frequently with his gun before he used it on you. The definitiveness of gun violence was most clearly shown in a major piece of research published by David Hemenway and Erin Richardson in 2007.[1] What they found was that our rate of assault hardly differed from assault rates in other advanced (OECD) countries, which was the evidence I was considering when I made the statement above about the generic quality of adolescent violence. But while the U.S. assault rate was similar to assault rates in countries like England, Germany, France and the like, our homicide rate was ten to *twenty times higher* than the homicide rates in those and other OECD countries because so many of our assaults involved the use of guns.

This year I went back and looked at the numbers again, because Hemenway's research did not extend beyond data from 2003. What I discovered was that the gap between our gun homicide rate and the average OECD rate remained unchanged even though both numbers declined by roughly 15 percent. Here is the way it looks on a country-by-county comparison as well as OECD and U.S. totals:[2]

Country	Pop. (000's)	Civilian Guns (000's)	Per Capita	Gun Hom. Rate
Australia	22,065	3,250	14.7	0.11
Austria	8,389	2,500	29.8	0.18
Canada	34,126	9,950	29.1	0.5
Czech Republic	10,519	136	1.2	0.12
Finland	5,363	2,400	44.7	0.26
France	65,031	19,000	29.2	0.22
Germany	81,776	25,000	30.5	0.2
Hungary	10,000	560	0.05	0.13
Iceland	315	90	28.5	0
Italy	60,463	7,000	11.5	0.36
Japan	127,450	710	0.005	0
Luxembourg	506	70	13.8	0.6
Netherlands	16,615	510	3	0.2
New Zealand	4,367	1,000	22.8	0.26
Norway	4,889	1,320	26.9	0.04
Portugal	10,637	2,600	24.4	0.48
Slovakia	5,430	450	8.2	0.18

Spain	46,070	4,500	9.7	0.15
Sweden	9,378	2,800	29.8	0.19
UK	62,271	4,060	6.5	0.05
TOTAL OECD	585,660	87,906	15	0.17
USA	309,326	270,000	87.2	3.58

The unanswered question, however, is not whether we have more homicides because we have more guns. That seems to me to be something of a no-brainer. The real question is: how come gun violence both in the OECD and the USA went down? This is truly the elephant in the living room when we try to figure out gun violence, or any violence for that matter, because the general decrease in these trends has never been satisfactorily explained. There are all kinds of theories floating around out there that seek to explain why we are killing ourselves both with and without guns at a steadily decreasing rate, and I discuss in some detail both the plausible and the absurd explanations in Volume I. But the problem continues to create issues both for understanding what is really going on with the issue of gun violence, as well as for figuring out what to do about solving the issue, if there's anything that can really be done.

Here's a case in point: the former New York City Mayor, Mike Bloomberg, has endowed a center on gun violence at The Johns Hopkins University that publishes extremely well-researched papers on various aspects of gun violence, most of them to provide the scholarly underpinning to gun control strategies that Bloomberg believes will, in fact, reduce deaths and all sorts of harm from guns. The group recently published a study that compared gun violence rates in Missouri before and after the state nullified a law in 2007 that previously had subjected all transfers of handguns, both through dealer and private channels, to a background check.[3] What the research uncovered was the fact that gun homicides increased substantially in the years directly after background checks were no longer required for private handgun sales. According to the Hopkins scholars, gun deaths increased nearly 25% from 2008 to 2012 (55 to 63 specific gun homicides) a trend that directly contradicts the research done by pro-gunners like John Lott (discussed in Chapter 2) who claim that gun violence goes down in jurisdictions where it becomes easier to carry a gun.

The work by the research team at Hopkins was thorough and detailed, but the attempt to tie changes in gun homicides to changes in the legal infrastructure covering access to guns gets stuck on one basic point. The fact is that at the same time that gun homicides were going up in Missouri, the overall homicide rate was going down, as was the rate of aggravated assaults. Between 2000 and 2007 the homicide rate fluctuated between 5.8 and 6.2 per 100,000, spiked to 7.7 in 2008 but then dropped back down to 6.1 in 2011. The aggravated assault rate reached 392 per 100,000 in 2007, but fell to 323 by 2012.

When one compares the gun homicide rate with the overall homicide rate and the overall physical violent crime rate, the difficulty of assigning some kind of rational relationship between gun violence and changes in the legal environment becomes clear. Because the fact is that if guns became a more favored way to commit violent crime, then overall homicide rates should have also increased, which they did not, or overall violent crime rates should have increased, which they did not, or robbery rates should have increased, which they did not. In fact, robbery rates remained remarkably stable during the entire period beginning in 2000 until they dropped significantly after 2007. If the absence of background checks for private handgun transfers made it easier for criminals and other unqualified individuals to get their hands on guns, there should have been some upward movement in other crime categories where guns are usually employed. In fact there was movement in all the other violent crime categories, except the movement wasn't up, it was down.

Here's the real problem and it's a discussion about this problem that I am going to use to end this book. It's clear that when we talk about gun violence we are talking about two types of behavior; one that winds up in a homicide and the other that winds up in a suicide. Now together these two types of gun violence account for less than 10% of all yearly gun violence events, but I think it's pretty obvious that the line between shootings that end in deaths and all other violence with guns, trigger pulled or not, is a line that's pretty fuzzy, pretty impulsive and pretty hard to pin down in terms of intent, motive, or any other way to look at this problem in rational terms. So let's just stick to the violence which ends up with a dead body and ignore, if you will, the dead bodies whose status is ruled as entirely accidental, because they never count for more than 3% of the gun deaths anyway, and we know exactly why these types of shooting occur—in case you haven't figured it out, it's something called stupidity or carelessness and it's no different than leaving the gate to the backyard pool unlocked the day your three-year-old toddled through the fence and—*kerplunk!*—ended up permanently floating face downward in the pool. Incidentally, there are more backyard drownings each year than accidental gun deaths anyway. Back to the homicides and the suicides, okay?

Notwithstanding much of my overheated rhetoric and sarcasm, I believe that most people who do research on guns are doing it from an honest and conscientious point of view. Every once in a while someone strays over the line and says something that simply doesn't make sense and I have done a pretty good job (I think) of discussing such efforts in Volume 1. But what happens to most gun researchers is that sooner or later most of them end up confusing coincidence with cause, the research about homicides in Missouri mentioned above being a typical case in point. It is simply inconceivable that a whole bunch of additional handguns would be floating around Missouri and the only category of violent crime that would experience an uptick is homicides, an uptick that took place at the same time that the crime category which is usually most sensitive to gun use—robbery—dropped way down. The contrast between those two trends simply flies in the face of reality if the only causal factor you can find to explain a spike in the number of gun homicides is an increase, or a possible increase in the number of illegally acquired guns. But here's why these flights from reality continue to abound in the scholarly and research literature about guns. Because the truth is that the behaviors that result in the most excessive form of gun violence—death—are perhaps the two most difficult types of behavior to understand, never mind analyze or explain.

It would be easier to analyze this problem if we experienced more or less the same level of gun violence year in and year out. But we don't. Or at least there have been periods and places where the change in gun violence rates have been so extreme that we can't simply ignore it or pretend that there's something going on for which a coincidental explanation is all we can advance at best. It may the case that national gun homicide rates have been more or less steady over the past decade and, in states like Missouri, actually going back up. But what cannot be ignored is that the rate of gun violence throughout the United States is still less than half of what it was in 1993. And this decline took place everywhere we look; in almost every state, in most large cities with inner-city, crime-ridden neighborhoods, in places where the cops got much more aggressive about looking for guns, in places where they did not. It took place where more people were allowed to carry concealed guns legally, it took place in places (like New York) where the idea of a legal concealed weapon is a contradiction in terms.

Which brings us to the next question: If most gun violence is the result of impulsive behavior, how come so many fewer impulsive people are walking around? Or to put it more specifically, how come there seem to be many less people who express their anger impulsively by using a gun? In Chapter 2 I reviewed the arguments of the NRA and their various factotums which attempts to prove that the impulse to use a gun has waned because there are so many people now walking around who would only use a gun in a proper and trained way and hence form a protective shield against the assholes who now can only bang away with their weapons If they can find a gun-free zone. And if I'm sounding a little sarcastic it's because these arguments are, as I stated earlier, built on whole cloth. But what doesn't come out of whole cloth is the undeniable fact that at least until 2008 the use of guns by civilians, impulsive or not, experienced a very substantial decline. And we still need to figure out why that decline in gun violence occurred.

Back to some numbers—quickly. The national homicide rate, as published by the FBI, was around 6 per 100,000 in the mid-60's. It then began climbing and reached its highest mark of 10.2 in 1980, remained just below that mark for the next decade and a half, and then began a steady decline after 1995:

Homicide Rate Per 100K

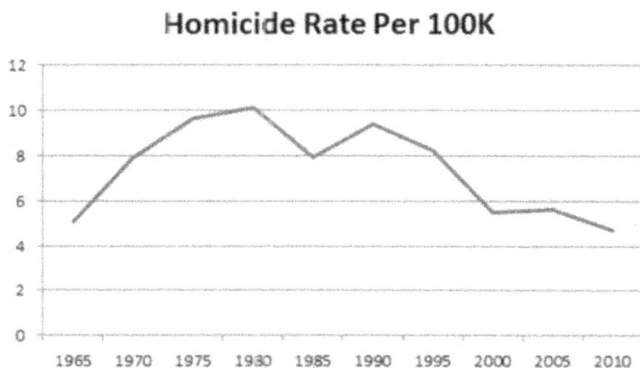

Although this graph covers all homicides, a graph covering gun homicides would look very similar because guns are used in roughly 65% to 75% of all homicides, year in and year out. And homicide trends tend to parallel other types of violent crimes involving guns such as robbery and aggravated assault, but the homicide numbers are usually somewhat more accurate because it's not that easy to hide a body, at least a body with a hole in it that was created by a bullet from a gun. The bottom line is that while the homicide rate and the overall violent crime rate seems to have nudged themselves slightly upward again in 2011 and 2012, we are still confronting a violent crime picture that zoomed upwards in the 1970s and again in the early 1990s, but has been receding ever since. How come?

I went over all the usual and not-so-usual theories about this issue in Volume 1 but there was one theory I didn't discuss at all. And that's because it's my theory and I was still doing the research on it when I wrote *Guns for Good Guys, Guns for Bad Guys*, and I needed a little more time and data in order to figure things out. But now I have finished the research so here goes.

Let's bring back the map that shows population density:

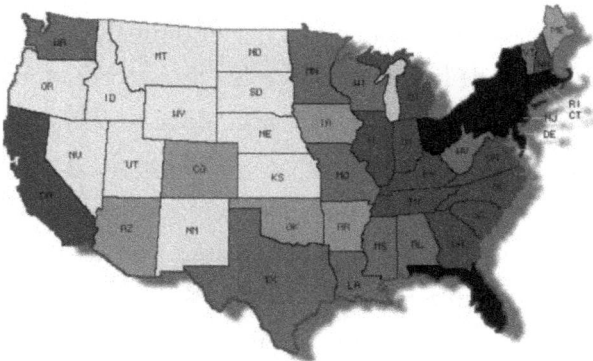

Notice that this map correlates pretty well with the map on aggravated gun assaults. And as I explained in Chapter 4, most gun use takes place in what we call metropolitan statistical areas, of which the larger ones tend to drive up the population density of the states in which they are found. But what I did not discuss in Chapter 4 was the fact that even in MSAs with overall high crime numbers there are usually great variations in gun use between different cities that share the same MSA, or even different neighborhoods that share the same city in the same MSA, or even different blocks or street-corners within the same neighborhood.

I am writing this chapter sitting in an office in the South End of Springfield, MA, and the office is located six blocks from a corner of Union Street where 4 and possibly 5 gun homicides occurred over the previous 15 months. The reason I am not sure if the homicide count from Union Street is 4 or 5 is because one of the victims whose body was found on Union Street may have been shot and killed somewhere else. Nobody saw nuttin,' as the old saying goes, so we'll probably never know for sure. Either way, there is absolutely no chance that I will face anyone holding a gun when I walk each morning from my car to my office or, alternatively, when I walk at the end of the day from my office to my car. But if I lived six blocks down Union Street and walked to and fro down that block, the odds that sooner or later I'd come up against some asshole with a banger in his hand are pretty high.

My office   Union Street Killing Ground

My theory about why gun violence has declined overall but why it is still so serious in certain places is based on the assumption that the only way to understand something as impulsive and inexplicable as gun violence is to understand what happens and what happened on the street-corner where it occurs. Because as I pointed out when I talked about Springfield's gun violence briefly in Volume 1 – *Guns for Good Guys,* there are many street-corners of this crime-ridden city in which no violent crime has ever taken place. Which is exactly the reason why so much of the analysis about gun violence, as I said at the beginning of this chapter, replaces causality with coincidence, because if a city has a high crime rate and a high rate of unemployment, for example, the fact that both go up doesn't mean that one happened because the other happened. Without knowing an exact number I can still say with great certainty that the unemployment rate on Union Street is very high. But according to the data from the U.S. Census Community Survey, the unemployment on the next street over, Quincy Street, is probably just as high because the rate in the whole neighborhood is high. Why haven't there been any murders on Quincy Street?

The way I am going to try to answer that question is to first look at the issue of gun violence not in terms of the relationship of attacker to victim, or the circumstances of their lives, or even the socio-economic circumstances of the neighborhood in which the violence occurs. Rather, I am going to assume that the real reason the violence takes place is due to the absence of certain involuntary and voluntary conditions that, if present, would make it more difficult, if not impossible, for such impulsive behavior to break out. Because violence, for certain individuals like a Ken McElroy from Whitmore, Missouri, might be normal behavior. It may also be normal and acceptable behavior for certain types of social or business associations like the Mafia or a drug cartel gang. But it's not a normal mechanism which most people can use to get through their daily lives or even just to move around. So at all levels, particularly the level of the neighborhood, the place where you spend most of your time because that's where you live, we develop these involuntary and voluntary mechanisms to keep things under control. And when these mechanisms don't function or don't function as well as they should, things get out of hand and sooner or later a dead body winds up in the street.

When I talk about involuntary mechanisms I am referring to the formalized organizations and practices that we create to control our behavior, whether we take part in the way in which such institutions operate or not. Schools and police are two perfect examples of involuntary mechanisms that we use to control behavior, because most people have nothing to do with them as long as they behave properly when the police come around on patrol or when they enter a school and sit down in a class. Mechanisms like police and schools exist to maintain certain norms of behavior, and when the police don't patrol properly or when too many kids drop out of the school, the behavior of the entire community served by those involuntary mechanisms tends to become worse.

Along with these involuntary mechanisms, most of which represent public (i.e., government) authority in one form or another, there are also voluntary mechanisms for maintaining neighborhood and community behavior, and it is the existence and operation of these mechanisms that really determines the degree to which a community can enforce proper behavior and protect itself from violence. Most of these voluntary mechanisms reflect the way in which people associate with other people within the neighborhood, sometimes on an organized basis such as a church congregation, sometimes on a more informal basis such as standing around the corner and simply talking to one another. I'll give you an example of the latter type of informal association from my own experience.

My grandparents owned a little produce (fruits and vegetables) store in a working-class neighborhood in Queens. By "working class" I mean that most of the people in the neighborhood rented their homes and apartments, which was not the usual situation in Queens where a majority of residents also owned the homes in which they lived. My grandparents' store was located on a commercial block that also had a drug store, a butcher, several notions and lotions shops, a beauty parlor, also known as a hair stylist, and a shoemaker. I'm talking about the 1950's, well before there was any kind of chain or franchise operation in this or other neighborhoods.

Most of the street traffic in the neighborhood consisted of people walking down the block to get to the subway station and commute into "da city" every day for work. Interspersed with the commuters, mostly male, were school-kids going to the grammar school around the corner or the junior high or high school that were located further away. After the morning "rush" was over the stores were frequented for the most part by housewives buying this or that for their homes, and then beginning in the late afternoon the morning traffic reversed itself and the sidewalks were crowded with kids coming home from school and men returning to the neighborhood from work.

My grandfather would begin closing his store around 5 P.M., as did all the other merchants on the block. Then at some point between 5:30 and 6 he would walk across the street and join a group of other men who virtually every day materialized around the drug store on the corner. Some of them had just come off the subway, others had already been home, perhaps eaten dinner and changed out of their suits and ties. But this group stood around in front of the drug store every day, and there were groups of men standing like this group on street-corners all over New York City at the same time.

Why were they standing there? Because they were waiting for the earliest edition of the next day's *Daily Mirror* newspaper to be dropped off for sale. The Mirror was a tabloid that competed, ultimately unsuccessfully, with the much more famous *New York Daily News,* the latter still being published in New York. The Mirror was always a little bit racier, a little sleazier in terms of headlines and pics, and its columnists like Westbrook Pegler tended to always find something just a little over the edge of respectability with which to titillate and excite their readership.

The men who gathered in front of the drug store, including my grandfather, weren't interested in the headlines, the pictures of various half-nude

Hollywood starlets or anything else. They were interested in learning one thing, the last 3 digits of that day's "handle," which was the amount of money bet on the Daily Double at the track. These three digits comprised the "number," and if you hit the number the return was 600 to 1. My grandfather bet a dime on the number five days a week and legend has it that he actually hit the number a couple of times which meant he came away with sixty bucks. And sixty bucks was a lot of money in 1954. It was probably more than what he earned in a week standing in his little fruit store and selling peaches for "one pound, twenty-nine." That's twenty-nine cents, by the way.

This group waiting to see if they hit the number might have been engaged in a bit of very petty criminality, but they didn't see it that way, and neither did the cop who patrolled that block and knew exactly why these guys were standing around the drug store. He also knew that while they were waiting for the truck that delivered the Daily Mirror, they also were his eyes and ears for the block. In a 2011 study of 25 urban sites, including large cities like Philadelphia, Houston, Los Angeles and Chicago, the 6-8PM time period was the highest for robberies in a majority of those cities. The 6-8PM period was even more frequent for assaults and was the highest rate time-period for all serious crimes combined, violent and property, for 15 of the 25 cities that comprised the study.

The one time I ever recall my grandparents expressing a fear of crime was after they came home from a trip into Manhattan on a Sunday afternoon and told me that they had been standing on a totally deserted subway platform in Midtown waiting for a train. My grandfather saw two men who looked "dangerous" (which meant they were black) walking towards him and my grandmother. He looked around, realized the platform was empty, took Mom by the arm and walked very quickly to the change booth and waited there for the train. I never heard him ever mention being afraid to walk home from the store. The neighborhood was safe and secure because there were all kinds of informal, voluntary mechanisms that existed and operated on the block, including a number of little old ladies who lived in the front ground floor apartments and seemed to spend all day at their windows gabbing with passer-bys or just looking up and down the street to see what was going on.

I wish I could say that that the idea of controlling crime and violent behavior through the existence and activity of these voluntary associations was my original theory, but it's not. It was developed by Jane

Jacobs in her remarkable book, *The Death and Life of Great American Cities,* and I wish the book were required reading for everyone and anyone who wants to talk about gun violence, because the way people behave in cities is influenced more than anything else by the physical and social contours of the neighborhoods in which people live. And I have tested her theory in the city I know best—New York City—and I have tested it using crime data that's about as close to street-level, incident-reported crime as you can get. The data I am referring to is crime data reported by each police precinct, and thanks to the generosity of several dedicated crime researchers whose names I will prominently mention in the notes at the end of this chapter, I can trace criminal patterns in virtually every New York City neighborhood going back twenty-five years.[4]

This quarter-century period, beginning in 1988, probably saw the greatest degree of neighborhood change in New York that took place in any twenty-five year period since bridges opened first from Manhattan to Brooklyn, then later when the subway went out to Queens. The dramatic changes in New York City neighborhoods after 1988 didn't take place, however, because the population grew in size. In fact, the city grew only by about one million residents, or by less than 15% at a time when the U.S. population increased by almost 30 percent. What happened in New York City, and happened in most larger cities during the same period, was a change in the *character* of many neighborhoods due to either gentrification or what I call re-urbanization, as well as a shrinking in the size of inner-city, minority neighborhoods due to the lessening of informal housing restrictions against racial minorities outside of the urban core.

The issue of crime and violence was never a factor in the wealthiest New York neighborhoods for several reasons. First, these neighborhoods tended to not only attract more formal protection from police, they also could afford to hire and deploy private resources, like apartment-house doormen and security guards to protect the neighborhood from the intrusions of criminal-prone people. Second, higher-end neighborhoods tended to restrict commercial enterprises to small and well-defined physical zones, therefore keeping street traffic to a minimum which only made it easier for private and public security forces to spot criminal elements. For example, the Upper East Side, the city's wealthiest neighborhood (and, for that matter, one of the wealthiest urban enclaves in the world), does not have a single commercial location of any kind—food store, boutique, pharmacy—for almost two miles between 59th and 96th Streets on Fifth Avenue; similarly Park

Avenue has exactly one small deli, a tailor and a tiny Chinese restaurant between 59th and 96th Streets. Pedestrian presence on these two, broad residential avenues is comprised almost exclusively either of residents or people visiting residents.

This neighborhood is protected by the 19th Precinct, whose territory contains slightly more than 200,000 residents. From 1988 until 1999 the 19th recorded an average of slightly more than 6 homicides a year, for a murder rate of 3 per 100,000. The national murder rate averaged above 8 during this period and New York City's murder rate until the last few years of this period was above 20. The same difference between crime in the 19th and the city-wide crime counts holds true for every other crime category, namely, that crime rates experienced by the wealthiest residents were less than one-third of what was going on in the rest of the city. And as crime throughout the city has declined over the past twenty-five years, this 1:3 ratio between crime and violence in the wealthiest neighborhoods compared to overall numbers has remained basically the unchanged.

Upper East Side – Park Avenue

Now let's go to the other extreme and take a look at one of the hard-core ghetto neighborhoods, Brooklyn's East New York. The area wasn't always an African American ghetto, in fact, it was mostly home before and after World War I to Italian and Jewish immigrants, and for the latter it served as the most densely populated Jewish neighborhood in all of New York. The original residents hung on into the 1950s, when their children began moving out to Queens and further to Long Island in the decades following World War II. It was also during the postwar years that New York's black population, most of whom had come from the South to the city during the Depression years, also began moving into this neighborhood but, as opposed to the earlier European-born immigrants and their children, this is where they stayed.

They stayed for two reasons. First and most important, the city began a slow economic decline during the 1960s that resulted in a substantial loss of jobs and income, in particular for inner-city blacks. The city's economy, which was previously based on small manufacturing operations employing less than 25 people, created plenty of semi-skilled jobs for minorities both within the manufacturing neighborhoods like the Garment District in Midtown Manhattan, as well as in the endless, petty commercial streets whose resilience reflected the size and strength of a localized, internal market that provided food, clothing and other daily consumables for an urban population that was more than twice as large as any other urban population and internal market within the United States. As small-scale manufacturing collapsed in New York City due to competition from lower-wage areas within the U.S. as well as from overseas, jobs particularly in the semi-skilled categories also quickly diminished or disappeared, and along with their disappearance went the local, neighborhood commercial activity that the wages from such semi-skilled jobs had previously kept afloat.

In addition to a decline in overall economic standards as whites fled the inner city and blacks could not find work was the insidious racism of the outer-borough neighborhoods and suburbs which had gradually opened up housing opportunities to European-born immigrants and their children, but drew the line when it came to Hispanics and blacks. And truth be told, much of this refusal to expand residential opportunities to racial minorities was a reflection of the desires of Jewish and Italian suburban residents who had run from inner-city neighborhoods precisely to avoid living in areas that were rapidly being filled with Puerto Ricans and blacks. My father, for example, grew up in the South Bronx, walking distance to Yankee Stadium, in a neighborhood that was nearly all-Jewish and virtually all-white until he left to go into the service in World War II. His two sisters both remained in the neighborhood during the war but then moved into neighborhoods on Long Island as soon as these areas began to accept Jews. And they were not at all bothered by the fact that where they now lived had been "restricted" for Jews in the years prior to the war, because they figured, as it turns out correctly, that such suburban enclaves would then remain off-limits to the Hispanics and blacks who moved into the apartments that they had vacated in the Bronx.

This pattern of former European immigrants or their descendants leaving the inner-city and being replaced by Hispanic and Blacks was repeated in neighborhood after neighborhood in the decades following the war. But by the time that neighborhoods like East New York were changing from white to Hispanic and black, they were also collapsing physically because the new residential population didn't have the economic resources to reclaim the housing stock that had been quickly and cheaply built for their predecessors and was now falling into decrepitude and decay. In the 1970s, New York City took ownership of over 60,000 housing units, many of them too far gone to provide adequate shelter on even the most minimal terms. In the place of these buildings the City constructed massive housing projects, basically small cities within the city, where minority residents who otherwise couldn't afford or find private housing options were allowed to live at sub-market rents. This basically meant that the poorest of the poor, with all the attendant social ills of poverty, were separated from normal neighborhood life which compounded and accelerated the collapse of these neighborhoods anyway.

Van Siclen Houses – Brooklyn. Picture by the author.

On the previous page is a picture of the Van Siclen Houses today in East New York. Compare it to the picture below of an East New York residential street taken in the 1930s:

Notice in the latter photo the small storefronts up and down the block. Not beautiful stores, not boutiques, but just enough commercial activity to give the block its own feel, its own sense of order, its own sense of control. The 1930's neighborhood is life-size, the apartment houses don't block out the sun or the sky. See anything comparable in the picture of the projects I took recently in East New York? Of course you don't. The neighborhood has disappeared.

This is exactly what happened in every inner-city neighborhood whose majority residents were Hispanic or black; it happened more obviously in black neighborhoods because Hispanics, particularly if their migration was of a more recent vintage and started someplace other than Puerto Rico, came to New York with more resources and, in many cases, with a petty entrepreneurial history and experience in the countries where they previously lived. But this was not true particularly of African-American neighborhoods, and the proof can be found in street-level crime data going back to the 1980's as well as today.

The 75th Precinct covers East New York, an area of roughly 4 square miles bounded by Atlantic Avenue to the North, Linden Boulevard to the South, Brownsville to the West and the Queens neighborhoods of Ozone Park and Woodhaven to the East. In 1988 this precinct recorded 5,869 violent crimes, or a rate per 100,000 of roughly 32. By 2008 the rate had fallen to 8.5, now it's back up to 10.6. In the 19th precinct, the violent crime rate today is less than 1; less than one-tenth what it is in East New York. But go directly across the Queens border into Woodhaven and the violent crime rate is 4.6. The two police precincts in East New York—the 75th—and Woodhaven—the 103rd—deploy 650 uniformed officers plus additional resources from various city-wide units like detectives, gang squad and so forth. But the per capita number of cops in East New York is 1 police for every 410 residents; in Woodhaven it's 1 cop for every 710. So the police presence is almost twice as high in East New York as it is in the neighboring area of Woodhaven, yet the violent crime rate in East New York is more than twice as high.

I thought that more cops was supposed to equal less crime. At least this is what Frank Zimring argues in the book he wrote, *The City That Became Safe*, that has become the standard explanation for why New York City has experienced the greatest drop in violent crime of any large city in the United States. Which, in fact, is true, if you look at crime data on an overall city basis. But that's exactly the whole point of understanding the relationship of behavior to neighborhoods. Because at the neighborhood level, reflected in the comparison between Woodhaven and East New York, the usual arguments about why crime and violence go up or go down, arguments based not on causality but coincidence, simply don't apply. After all, the fact that East New York is located in the borough of Brooklyn and Woodhaven is located in the borough of Queens is nothing other than an administrative quirk having to do with the history and politics of the settlement of the city. Walk underneath the Van Wyck Expressway and on the southbound side you're in Brooklyn and on the northbound side you're in Queens. The difference in violence between East New York and Woodhaven has nothing to with the political boundaries that separate these two neighborhoods; it has everything to do with how these neighborhoods have changed.

At the two extremes, the wealthiest and the most disadvantaged, the neighborhoods in New York that fit into these categories have changed little, if at all. The "best" zip codes, like 10021 and 10028 on Manhattan's Upper East Side, were always mostly vertical and remain that way. Some new buildings have sprouted close to the East River and along the 86th Street commercial corridor, but the older hi-rises that occupy most of Fifth, Madison and Park Avenues remain the residential anchors of the neighborhood and set the tone. The poorest zip codes, like Brooklyn's 11208 and 11207 in East New York, were always largely horizontal, and with the exception of the ghostly (or ghastly) public housing towers, they remain horizontal or abandoned and swept away altogether today.

What is remarkable about the ghetto is its lack of population and its open space. East New York has a population density about half the density of Manhattan's Upper East Side; vacant space is at a premium (basically non-existent) in the less than 4 square miles bounded by Central Park on one side, the East River on the other, going north from 59th Street to 96th. Roughly the same amount of real estate in East New York, bounded by Linden, Atlantic,

Pennsylvania and Conduit Avenues contains mega-amounts of undeveloped parcels, sometimes hidden behind wooden fences, sometimes used for off-street parking in an informal kind of way, sometimes sitting there with no sign of access or use at all.

Glenmore Avenue in East New York – picture by author.

The great change in urban neighborhoods, both in New York City and urban centers throughout the United States, has come about for two reasons: gentrification and what I call re-urbanization. The former usually either applies to neighborhoods whose middle-class residents resisted the socio-economic erosion that took place in working class neighborhoods whose residents cut free and ran to the 'burbs, or former industrial and warehousing neighborhoods, often waterfront locations, that were revamped and reinvigorated through a combination of private development and public aid. An example of such waterfront gentrification is the High Line park and development zone that runs along Manhattan's lower west side. This area, on the edge of a neighborhood known as Chelsea, used to be home to meatpacking plants, warehouses holding goods unloaded from ships and ferries that docked on Hudson River piers, flophouses and transient hotels for merchant mariners and salesmen, and crummy, run-down tenement apartments that housed the dock workers and laborers who serviced the trains and ships that transported goods in and out of the urban zone.

When I lived in Manhattan in the late 1980's, this area had a few meatpacking plants and a bit of warehousing but for the most part it was commercially dead. At night it was completely deserted except for the few hookers who plied their trade under elevated train tracks that had formerly been used by the Grand Central Railroad to haul cargo away from the piers or shift large amounts of goods from one storage location to another. Nobody remembers the exact date at which this elevated track and the buildings around it fell into disuse, but I hiked about a mile of this abandoned track in 1985 and from the amount of litter and the height of the weeds it clearly had not seen any activity for several decades at the very least.

Construction of the High Line Park commenced in 2006 and was completed by 2011. By the time the park was completed, the residential area surrounding this mile-long investment in urban gentrification had turned into the city's most exciting destination both for tourists and city residents alike. Trendy restaurants, clubs, boutiques and hotels compete for street-front space, luxury apartment residences are being built at a record pace, an area that had been dark and deserted both during the daytime and at night is now a bonanza in terms of real estate rates, restaurant prices and, most of all, pedestrian traffic, activity and lively noise. This type of planned gentrification has happened in waterfront neighborhoods all over the United States. You can find it along the riverfront in Philadelphia, which used to be just as dilapidated and run down as the waterfront in New York. You can even experience a lovely waterfront afternoon in a third-tier city like Fargo, whose downtown park alongside the Red River has attracted a new class of gourmet restaurants and trendy boutiques. We're talking about Fargo, North Dakota, not Manhattan.

The gentrification of middle-class, urban neighborhoods has also been spurred by the decision of younger city residents to resist the lure of the suburbs and instead to remain in the urban environment to work and raise their kids. Many of these families consist of two wage-earners working in high-wage occupations like finance or IT. They can afford top-tier housing costs, private schools and fat restaurant tabs because the convenience and attractions of city life outweigh the alleged advantages of suburban life. The 2010 census marked the very first time that cities began growing faster than suburbs and it was recently estimated by Brookings that population growth in the central cities of America's 51 metropolitan areas with populations in excess of 1 million outpaced suburban growth overall by 1.1 to .9 percent from 2010 to 2012.

These gentrified neighborhoods are increasingly resistant to violence and crime. The 10th Precinct, which covers Chelsea and the High Line, recorded 9 homicides in 1991 and 8 homicides in 1999. Between those two years, homicides throughout the city had dropped by nearly 50 percent. In Chelsea they hadn't declined at all. The High Line opened in 2006 and in 2007, and for the first time since 1988, there were no murders in this precinct and 1 murder was committed in 2013. There has been an uptick over the last several years in property crimes, particularly burglary and car theft, not surprising in an area that now experiences massive amounts of transient automobile traffic throughout the night. But the overall violent crime rate continues to slide downward even though throughout the city it has been moving up slightly since 2010, and this trend in the 10th precinct can be found in other neighborhoods that have gentrified as well.

The much more important change that has taken place in many New York neighborhoods and urban neighborhoods across the country is a process I refer to as re-urbanization, which is the rescue of what otherwise were becoming increasingly marginal neighborhoods by the settlement of a new wave of immigration coming to the U.S. from the Pacific Rim, Southeast Asia, the Indian subcontinent, former Soviet territories, Central and Latin America, and even parts of Central Africa. The appearance of this large and diverse immigrant population is most evident in New York because it is still the major point of entry into the country, but it is happening in every major city in the United States.

In New York, foreign-born residents number more than 3 million, the highest number since the period of the Great Migration, before and after World War I. The largest single group is Dominican, followed closely by immigrants from China, then Mexico, Jamaica, Guyana, Haiti, Trinidad, India and

Russia. The last two groups alone count more than 150,000 city residents. These new immigrants have settled throughout the city (Staten Island, which had always been the borough with the least number of foreign-born residents, saw a jump of nearly 40% in immigrants over the last ten years), but in particular they tend to favor Brooklyn and Queens, the latter which previous to the arrival of this population was considered the least ethnically and culturally diverse of all four major boroughs.

Here's a map of the city's neighborhoods with the darker areas denoting higher numbers of new immigrants and next to it is a map showing crime rates throughout the city (darker = more crime).

Pct. of immigrants (darker = higher)   Violent crime rates (darker = higher)

Notice something interesting? The areas in Queens and Brooklyn that have the lowest crime rates (no shading) are also, in most cases, the areas with the highest concentration of new immigrants. In Brooklyn these are neighborhoods like Bushwick and Bensonhurst; in Queens it's a belt that runs from Flushing and Jackson Heights down through Forest Hills. The immigrant communities that have settled in these neighborhoods are, as opposed to the European-born immigrants of earlier decades, committed to staying within the urban environment, and much of this commitment is due to the degree that they have revitalized local commerce and economic activity through a combination of sidewalk retail and small-shop manufacture and merchandising. If nothing else, this pattern of starting up small, entrepreneurial enterprises not only keeps a large part of the active immigrant population within the local community, but also makes them more concerned with quality of life issues at the street-corner level. Which means a commitment to the types of voluntary social associations and mechanisms which inhibit violent behavior and crime.

The striking thing about these new immigrant neighborhoods, in addition to the polyglot of foreign languages and cultural expressions, is the degree to which the sidewalks are always active and crowded day and night, as opposed to both wealthy and impoverished areas which, more than anything, are so often deserted at times when you would expect people to be around. While newly gentrified neighborhoods also display a great deal of street and pedestrian traffic, most of these people are visitors from outside the area while the proportion of locals intermixed with the tourists is often quite slight. In re-urbanized neighborhoods, on the other hand, the non-residents immediately stand out, particularly if they represent a different ethnic or racial group from those that settled on that particular block.

In neighborhoods where new immigrants are most intensely settled, crime rates tend to be the lowest, and more important, violent crime as a proportion of all crime is always lower than the proportion of violent crimes in the city as a whole. Over the quarter-century from 1988 to 2013, violent crime has been 31% of all crime reported by the NYPD. The percentage has dropped slightly over the last ten years, but in ghetto neighborhoods like Brownsville, East New York and Bed-Stuy, violent crimes still account for at least half of all crimes, whereas in re-urbanized neighborhoods like Woodhaven, Flushing and Bensonhurst, violent crime is less than 20 percent. The residents of these neighborhoods aren't just depending on the police to keep them safe from the random impulses of violence that break out in other, less-safe urban zones. They are depending on themselves to control neighborhood behavior and to make sure that their shops, their street-corners, their playgrounds and their parks are protected from violence and crime. I do not possess data beyond New York, but I am told that there has been a similar displacement of violent crime in new immigrant neighborhoods in Los Angeles, and I suspect it would be found in new immigrant neighborhoods all over the United States.

I think the issue of violence, and gun violence in particular, has to be understood not in terms of why it doesn't happen but why it does. And I don't mean this in terms of socio-economic factors (poverty, unemployment, rootlessness) that might create conditions in which this type of behavior takes place. I mean it in terms of whether or not the individual who engages in this behavior knows that what he is doing should not be done. And the reason he knows it is because at the moment he's about to do it, there is someone else around whose presence makes him realize that his violent behavior is over the line. Maybe it's the person against whom he would engage in the behavior, maybe it's a foe or a friend. But at the moment he loses control and surrenders to the impulse to behave in an angry way, there's nobody else around to hold him back. That's what happens in the 19,000 instances of gun violence which occur each year when someone pulls out a gun and aims it at themselves. It would have happened to my friend, the retired cop, except that someone walked into his living room and her presence made him realize that he could not cross that line.

I believe the same thing holds true when we are talking about the impulse which results in someone aiming a gun at someone else. There was another murder last year in the same town down the road from where I live where the two assholes killed the old man. In this case a third asshole, also in his early 20s, broke into the home of an old lady whom he thought had gone out, but instead found her asleep in her living-room couch and bashed her over the head. He had previously been picked up multiple times as a suspect in residential B&E's that had taken place around town, and his modus operandi was to spot homes lived in by older people, stand around and wait for them to leave their residences to go shopping or take care of some other chore, then break in through a back door or window, grab loose cash that was lying around and take off. He knew enough not to steal jewelry or other possessions because in a small town such items, when pawned, could easily be traced. He also had never engaged in any kind of violent behavior, or at least none that was reported as a crime. He had a girlfriend with whom he lived in the next town, and he managed by dint of his break-ins to avoid any other form of work.

In this particular instance he was caught because a detective assigned to the case noticed a cigarette butt that had been crushed out on the sill of the window that appeared to have been opened and through which the kid had gained entrance to the victim's home. The old lady lived across the street from the local hospital and usually went across to the hospital each morning to volunteer as a docent in the department of patient care. This morning she evidently stayed home or just decided to get a little more sleep and she was sleeping so soundly that the burglar didn't awaken her when he smashed the back window and lifted himself into her home. It was also clear that she did not wake up nor offer any resistance before the kid decided to do her in. In other words, she slept through the entire invasion and looting of her home. And it was also clear that the kid, once he realized how soundly she was sleeping, went through and ransacked every room.

He was identified several months later from the DNA of the cigarette butt and was arrested while he was sitting with his girlfriend on his front porch. He offered no resistance, at first tried a weak alibi, and never admitted to being inside the home. Why was there a cigarette butt with his DNA on the window that had obviously been smashed in order for someone to gain entrance into the home? He didn't know and he couldn't remember whether he had ever been in the home or not. And while the murder weapon was never recovered, it was assumed to be a metal pipe or bar of which there were a few others lying under the kitchen sink because a plumber several months' earlier had come in and done some repairs.

I asked the police chief to explain this case to me and, as in the other murder he was very pleased that one of his officers had alertly responded and they were able to figure it out. But in this case they figured out the who, the what and the where but not the why. "Another asshole" was the chief's response when I asked him how come a young kid felt he had no choice but to bash in the head of an old widow. Why didn't this asshole pull a gun out of his pocket and shoot the woman to death rather than bang her over the head with a pipe? If he couldn't control or even explain the impulse to kill her, why not use a gun? Because he didn't have one. Like Walter Mosley says, "If you carry a gun, it's bound to go off sooner or later."

He's right.

Notes to Chapter 6

1. Supra, fn. 8, Chapt. 1.

2. Data on non-U.S. gun ownership from UNODC, "2011 Global Study on Homicide," supra.

3. This article will shortly appear in Journal of Urban Health. I worked off the press release summary credited to Daniel Webster at the Bloomberg Center.

4. The 1988-2001 precinct data was graciously sent to me by Professor Robert Fornango at Arizona State University. Cf., Fornango, Rosenfeld & Rengifo, "The Impact of Order-Maintenance Policing on New York City Homicide and Robbery Rates: 1988-2001, Criminology, 45, 2 (2007), 355-384. On New York City crime, also see, "David F. Greenberg, "Studying New York City's Crime Decline; Methodological Issues, Justice Quarterly, 31:1, 154-188; B. Bowling, "The Rise and Fall of New York Murder: Zero Tolerance or Crack's Decline?" British Journal of Criminology, 39, 4 (Autumn, 1999), 531-554; Michael White, "The New York City Police Department, its Crime-Control Strategies and Organizational Changes, 1970-2009." Graciously sent to me by the author who is Associate Professor at Arizona State University.

FURTHER READING AND ACKNOWLEDGEMENTS

Following Sandy Hook there was a spate of gun books published, as everyone wanted to get into the debate while the debate was going on. I am not sure that any of the books told us anything really new or different about guns, gun violence, or any other related subject. But if you do not have a background in this literature, the following works will at least help fill the gap:

Tom Diaz, The Last Gun, How Changes in the Gun Industry are Killing Americans and What It Will Take to Stop It. (New York, 1913.)

Craig R. Whitney, Living with Guns, A Liberal's Case for the Second Amendment (New York, 2012).

On violence you can find comprehensive discussions and references to scholarship in, Flannery, Vazsonyi & Waldman, eds., The Cambridge Handbook of Violent Behavior and Aggression (Cambridge, 2007).

A more specific approach is David Kennedy, Don't Shoot – One Man, A Street Fellowship and The End Of Violence in Inner-City America (New York, 2011).

On the decline of violence and crime in the United States, see Franklin Zimring, The Great American Crime Decline (New York, 2007) and Blumstein & Wallman, eds., The Crime Drop in America (New York, 2000.)

To gain a proper perspective on gun violence, I suggest you read the following works: David Hemenway, Private Guns, Public Health (Ann Arbor, 2004). A thoughtful and comprehensive analysis of gun violence from the scholarly and applied perspectives.

Graduate Institute of International and Development Studies, Small Arms Survey, published annually since 2001.

I wish to thank the following for their help, advice and good cheer: Chris Barsotti, Megan Ranney, Robert Fornango, Catherine Barber, Carolyn and Lennard the Cat.

ABOUT THE AUTHOR

Michael R. Weisser was born in Washington, D.C., educated in New York City public schools and received a Ph.D. in Economic History at Northwestern University. He is a featured blogger with Huffington Post and also blogs about guns at www.mikethegunguy.com. Since 1978 he has been a firearms retailer, wholesaler, law enforcement distributor and importer with total gun sales in excess of 30,000 handguns, rifles and shotguns. He is also a Life Member of the NRA and a certified firearms instructor in six specialties. He can be reached at his blog or at mike@mikethegunguy.com.